Understanding Police Use of Force

by

Howard Rahtz

Criminal Justice Press
Monsey, New York
2003

ISBN 10: 1-881798-42-9
ISBN 13: 978-1-881798-42-2

Cover design by Laurey Lebenson.

Contents

This book is dedicated to the staff of the Cincinnati Police Academy, who every day demonstrate the integrity, commitment and professionalism that make policing a great profession. And to my family — Kathy, Denny, Christine, and Caroline. They always keep it in perspective.

Preface

Following the riots in Cincinnati in April of 2001, I found myself at meeting after meeting where the discussion started with "How did this happen here?" It was a difficult question. Cincinnati is not and was not the racist "Belly of the beast" as described with hyperbolic fury by NAACP leader Kweisi Mfume. Cincinnati certainly has the same sort of problems afflicting most big cities in America. And by some measures, Cincinnati was better off than many other cities. The police department, vilified in the local and national press, had just been reaccredited by the Commission for Law Enforcement Accreditation (CALEA), a process that put the department in compliance with the highest standards established for law enforcement agencies. The department's use-of-force rate, by the best figures available, was well below the national average. In a 2001 *Washington Post* study of fatal police shootings in the 50 largest jurisdictions in the country, Cincinnati police shootings were among the lowest.

Cincinnati was a city where the economy was good, the unemployment rate and the crime rate were low, and the United Appeal always met its goal. City schools had the same problems as most big city systems, but by test scores and other indicators, the system was the best urban district in the state. Much of the city talk revolved around the local sports teams, and racial tensions in the town were submerged under layers of mid-western conservatism and politeness.

After the riots, none of that mattered. In most people's minds, the riots stemmed either from police action or the criminal element in the street, and the community split up, largely along racial lines, in support of the police or against them.

Many of the community meetings I attended, organized by clergy and social service agencies, tended to focus on "what's wrong with the cops?" Much of the dialogue was emotional, and even as the immediate wave of anger and hostility subsided, the thrust of the discussion was still on how to fix the police department. Police use of force always generated heated debate, and it quickly became apparent to me that the level of public knowledge about every aspect of the issue was weak at best. The few police officers in attendance left disappointed and concerned about the gap in understanding that separated us from the others who were there.

The issue crystallized for me when several weeks later a team including "policing experts" from the U.S. Department of Justice (DOJ) visited the Cincinnati Police Academy to review our training. The discussion quickly turned to training for use of force. "Show me your use-of-force lesson plans," a young DOJ attorney demanded.

"Can you be more specific?" I asked. "Use of force is woven throughout the curriculum. It's in firearms training, defensive tactics, legal issues, ethics — in fact, every area we teach in has a connection to use of force."

It was clear that was not the answer he was looking for, and he suggested our failure to have a huge volume of lesson plans stamped "Use of Force" was a clear deficiency. The discussion grew spirited from there. We debated on when mace was appropriate, when restraining someone became force, and whether it was ever okay for the cops to "get in their cars and leave" when a situation began to deteriorate. Much of the disagreement was among the "experts," and it became apparent that even within the police community there are a wide range of opinions on every aspect of police force.

It struck me that some dialogue between citizens and police on the issue of use of force is overdue. That sort of discussion rarely occurs and when it does, usually in the aftermath of a crisis, the finger-pointing and blaming that passes for dialogue doesn't really help the community or the police.

Police use-of-force incidents can have drastic consequences for all of us — the officer, the citizen involved, and the community at large. The stakes are too high for police officers and citizens to continue to talk past each other. If we can begin to find some common ground on force issues, these incidents will be less likely to tear at the fabric of our community life. It's my hope that this book can make a small contribution to that dialogue.

Howard Rahtz
Cincinnati, Ohio
March 10, 2003

Foreword

Policing is an anomaly in democratic countries. Police agencies, as Egon Bittner pointed out years ago, have a monopoly on the legitimate use of force in societies that, in most other respects, disdain force as a tool of individual or collective policy. I am prohibited from exacting personal vengeance on a neighbor who takes my property or causes injury to my family or myself. In return, I am assured that an agency of government, the police, will see to it that my personal injustice is addressed. The logic of this is apparent when we observe situations in which people feel they cannot call upon a neutral police agency. People who routinely engage in illegal behavior, such as drug dealers, must either suffer repeated victimization, or take matters into their own hands. The result is the high rate of assaults and killings among such individuals.

Giving the police the exclusive power to use force confers a certain status upon the police. But it makes the police and their actions suspect. As the founder of modern democratic policing, Robert Peel, stated in his nine principles,

> Police, at all times, should maintain a relationship with the public that gives reality to the historic tradition that the police are the public and the public are the police; the police being only members of the public who are paid to give full-time attention to duties which are incumbent on every citizen in the interests of community welfare and existence.

This is, of course, a simple extension of the fact that the police are a part of democratic government, itself an extension of the public. However, having a monopoly on the legitimate use of force sets the police apart from common citizens and other government agents. The police are not simply doing what citizens or bureaucrats would otherwise do. They are also exercising a capacity that is denied common citizens and other governmental employees. So the monopoly on legitimate use of force requires the police to give special attention to how they are perceived by the public.

Public perception of the police is colored by their use of force. When force is used, the public and elected officials demand that its use be justified. And as Robert Peel also noted in his principles, "The degree of co-operation of the public that can be secured diminishes proportionately to the necessity of the use of physical force."

So though police are endowed with the ability to use force, their effectiveness is diminished by its use. Force is an asset whose power declines through use. A threat that needs to be carried out is not particularly credible. But if force is required and the police fail to use it, the public and elected officials are quick to ask why the police did not use force. Clearly the police cannot be seen as using too much or too little force. And like all middle grounds, there are no bright warnings showing what is too much or too little.

Cincinnati has recently become an involuntary laboratory for exploring the complex interaction between police use of force and police legitimacy. Over the last six years, this city has witnessed the deaths of police officers at the hands of citizens and the deaths of citizens at the hands of police. It has been the scene of a riot in neighborhoods in which the police were accused of using too much force, and it has been the scene of riots by college students in which the police were accused of using too little force. And as one might expect, race is an important confounding factor in this recent history.

Understanding police use of force is simple, if one is willing to overlook its complexities. At first blush, it appears to be simply a matter of law. But as Howard Rahtz shows in this book, the law provides only broad guidance. For example, relatively recent U.S. Supreme Court decisions rule out the use of deadly force to stop a fleeing suspect who does not appear to be an immediate threat. But when officers determine that there are immediate threats to themselves or others, courts have been reluctant to second-guess them. When it comes to other uses of force, understanding the law is only the beginning.

Over the last half century, there has been a trend toward curbing police use of force. And it is not too much of a stretch to claim that this is largely due to the civil rights movement in the

United States. If each of us is safer from unwarranted police intrusion into our actions, then we have civil rights leaders to thank. But we also should thank many within the ranks of the police. Much of the recent progress toward circumscribing police use of force has focused on administrative changes, under the control of the police, such as improved training, early warning systems, discipline procedures and strategic changes in policing, such as community policing. The expansion of these controls is due in no small measure to the work of police practitioners.

Public condemnation of police use of force does not differentiate between police officials who find the acts appalling and those who believe them to be justified. While news media stories often pit the police against the public (particularly the non-white public), they seldom describe the debates within policing over what acts constituted prudent use of force, and under what circumstances. By bringing an insiders view to these complex, uncertain, and highly charged issues Howard Rahtz has made a tremendous contribution to the public discussion on police use of force.

John E. Eck, Ph.D.
Division of Criminal Justice
University of Cincinnati

Chapter 1. Understanding the Gap

"Other than random attacks, all such cases (excessive force) begin with the decision of a police officer to do something, to help, to arrest, to inquire. If the officer had decided to do nothing, then no force would have been used. In this sense, the police officer always causes the trouble. But it is trouble which the police officer is sworn to cause..."

Plakas v. Drinski (1993)

It is always an ugly story. Whether it's the videotaped beating of Rodney King, 41 shots fired by New York police officers in the Amadou Diallo death, or a single shot killing an unarmed teenager in Cincinnati, police use of force is perhaps the most contentious issue in our country. When these incidents play out in the context of American racial politics, community polarization and strained police-community relations result.

Consider some recent news reports:

Los Angeles, California — On October 28, 2000, LAPD Officer Tarriel Hopper and his partner responded to a loud noise complaint stemming from a Halloween party. As they approached a rear window of the home, Anthony Dwain Lee, who was in costume, reportedly turned toward the officers and pointed a fake gun at them. Hopper fired several shots through the window killing Lee. Lee's family has filed a $100 million lawsuit against the city. The incident remains under investigation ("LAPD Hit Again," 2000).

Providence, Rhode Island — The Providence Police Department plans to conduct extensive background checks on its applicants in an effort to eliminate potential bias on the force. The checks were recommended by a state committee formed after the

2000 fatal shooting of Sgt. Cornell Young Jr., an off-duty black police officer who was accidentally shot by two white patrolmen. A grand jury cleared the two officers of wrongdoing, but the shooting sparked accusations of racism from across the state ("PD to Check...," 2001).

Minneapolis, Minnesota — A Minneapolis neighborhood erupted in violence after a 10-year-old African-American boy was injured in a police shooting. The boy was wounded when an officer shot at a pit bull that attacked the officer while he was serving a search warrant. The shot missed the dog, ricocheted off concrete and struck the boy in the arm ("Minneapolis Mayor...," 2002).

Boston, Massachusetts — Black leaders supported a policy change prohibiting officers from firing at moving cars, while police union members demanded the resignation of Police Commissioner Paul Evans, who pushed through the change. The policy dispute follows a police shooting in which a Dorchester woman became the eighth person killed by Boston Police in the last 22 months. The woman was a backseat passenger in a car that allegedly attempted to strike an officer and then sped away ("Black Leaders...," 2002).

San Francisco, California — A burglary suspect died after being "pepper-sprayed" and handcuffed by SFPD officers, including Officer Marc Andaya. Despite a coroner's ruling that the suspect died of acute cocaine poisoning, Officer Andaya's history generated media attention to the case. Andaya had previously been employed by the Oakland Police Department, where he had amassed more than 30 citizen complaints and a supervisory review that complained about "cowboy" behavior. Andaya was subsequently fired for lying on his application to the SFPD (Gordon, 1995).

Portland, Oregon — Portland officers responded to reports of unruly men on a city bus. Two officers ended up firing 27 shots at one of the men, Gerald Gratton, as he fled from the bus. At the time of the incident, Gratton had a gun tucked in his waistband, but he did not pull it during the incident. One of the officers involved, Douglas Erickson, fired 23 shots at Gratton. Erickson was terminated after the city's investigation concluded that Gratton had not posed an imminent threat to the officers or citizens. Erickson took his firing to arbitration and was ordered reinstated with back pay. The arbitrator ruled Erickson's actions represented "faulty tactical judgment" not deserving of job loss. The local media thought otherwise. An editorial in the local paper stated, "The arbitrator's conclusion that faulty tactical judgment by a police officer does not justify his dismissal on grounds of unjustified use of deadly force demonstrates extraordinary legalistic tunnel vision. The ruling screams for reanalysis of the rules by which police performance is judged in this city" (*Oregonian*, 1995).

Charlotte, North Carolina — Members of the Charlotte Police Complaint Review Program decided not to review a fatal police shooting that occurred on September 15, 2001. Troy Johnson "pepper-sprayed" three Charlotte officers during a traffic stop, then fled to a nearby apartment. Johnson fought with six officers in the apartment prior to being shot to death by Officer Greg Hester. Johnson had an extensive criminal history and had cocaine and alcohol in his system at the time of his death. The 11-member citizen review panel was formed in 1997 and has reviewed 32 cases to date, supporting the police on each incident. The local office of the FBI is investigating the case (Moore, 2002).

Cincinnati, Ohio — Rioting followed the shooting of Timothy Thomas in April of 2001. Thomas, wanted on multiple misdemeanor warrants, ran when confronted by police and was shot by a Cincinnati officer, who stated that Thomas was pulling at his waistband for what the officer believed was a weapon. The disorder began at a raucous City Council meeting where hundreds of protesters jammed the council chambers (Horn, 2001).

Louisville, Kentucky — Demonstrators marched to Police Headquarters to protest the shootings of blacks by Louisville Police. The marchers wanted a civilian review board established in the city, a move opposed by the Louisville Mayor Dave Armstrong (Holbrook, 2001).

Tulsa, Oklahoma — An arbitrator ordered two Tulsa officers reinstated after finding there was no evidence the two used excessive force during an off-duty incident in April of 2000. The two officers, a married couple, Buddy and Lori Visser, made an off-duty traffic stop after someone threw something at them from the vehicle. The officers pointed their guns at the car's occupants, but no charges were filed against the occupants. Tulsa Police Chief Ron Palmer was upset with the arbitrator's action, stating, "I can't be more in disagreement with the ruling." A civil suit against the officers has been filed ("Accused of...," 2001).

Des Moines, Iowa — Police are promising to change their tactics after admitting they mishandled a raid at a cafe in which 10 innocent people, mostly Asian, were handcuffed. "What we intend to do is look at training, the decisions the officers made, and see if there is a better way to analyze the challenge they had before them, then come up with better tactics," Police Chief William Moulder said. Assistant Police Chief William McCarthy started meeting with officers to evaluate their training and consider changing how they approach such situations. McCarthy said the tactics make sense at the police academy, but may not to the average person. "When push comes to shove, it's the citizens who are judging us, not the police academy," he said ("Police Announce...," 2001).

Tucson, Arizona — A citizen board of inquiry criticized Tucson police for their response to rioting that followed the University of Arizona's defeat in the 2001 NCAA Basketball Tournament. The board claimed the police did not take precautions to distinguish peaceful students leaving the arena and those involved in the rioting. Police fired over 300 "less than lethal" rounds during the disturbance. The board upheld three specific instances of excessive force, and one student has filed a $3 million lawsuit for loss of an eye after being hit with one of "less than lethal" projectiles ("Tucson Board...," 2001).

Inglewood, California — Jeremy Morse, a three-year Inglewood officer, was under investigation for a videotaped incident involving a handcuffed 16-year-old African American who was slammed on the hood of a car and then punched in the face by Morse. Officer Morse was subsequently fired and is facing a criminal assault charge. The incident attracted national attention, and the family filed a federal lawsuit less than a week after the incident. "We believe this is a seven-figure case," said the family's attorney John Sweeney (Tong, 2001).

Detroit, Michigan — Detroit Police Officer David Krupinski was found innocent of a manslaughter charge for the shooting death of Edwin Shaw on August 29, 2000. Shaw was deaf and was brandishing a rake at officers at the time of the shooting. Family members and friends contended that the rake had never left Shaw's shoulder, but other officers on the scene said Shaw was swinging the rake toward another Detroit Officer when Krupinski opened fire. The shooting and subsequent trial of Krupinski received national attention. The U.S. Department of Justice is currently probing a number of shootings, including Shaw's, by Detroit Police (Hanson, 2001).

*   *   *   *

Several themes run through these incidents. How are police trained to use force? What is justifiable force and how do we judge individual incidents? Should police be using force when they are off-duty? Why don't police use non-lethal weapons? Can't they shoot people in the arms or legs rather than killing them? Are police profiling minorities? Is there a problem with the police culture and can police departments be trusted to police themselves? Should there be more citizen oversight? Do police officers need more diversity training? How do officers with a history of brutality and citizen abuse stay on the job?

In the aftermath of a deadly-force incident and under the intense glare of the media, police training, police use-of-force policies, and citizen complaints of excessive force are aired and dissected. Cops are quick to point out that use-of-force decisions are often made in a split-second and it is unfair for the average person on the street to reach a judgment about them over the morning newspaper. Most citizens are supportive of the police, but skeptical about the ability of police to investigate themselves.

Skepticism on police use of force is most pronounced when racial minorities are the target of the force and the police officers involved are white. Many leaders and members of minority communities believe the police are too quick to resort to force — especially deadly force — against non-whites, particularly African Americans. Racial profiling and racism are believed by many Americans to be part of the police culture, and they judge force incidents in that context.

At least part of the problem is a lack of a community consensus on a framework and language for review and discussion of police use of force. What exactly is force? How do cops determine what force to use in each situation? How do officers' perceptions of reasonable and excessive force differ from the general public's? And what role, if any, does the race of the officer or the race of the citizen play in these incidents?

This "language" dilemma is more than an academic exercise. Without more precise understanding of this core function of policing, officers, and citizens as well, have no standards by which to measure police performance. Exemplary police work becomes barely distinguishable from incompetence and brutality.

We can do better.

Discussion Questions

(1) Think of a police use-of-force incident, either national or local. What about that situation went right and what went wrong? How would your friends describe the incident? How would you describe the incident?

(2) What role do you believe race plays in police use of force? Is there any evidence that police officers, regardless of their ethnicity, use force more often against people of other races?

(3) List the personal qualities you want to see in the police officers in your neighborhood. How does this description fit with the fact that police officers have the authority and responsibility to use force against citizens?

Chapter 2. Use of Force:
Definitions and Data

"In fact, our expectation that policemen will use force, coupled by our refusals to state clearly what we mean by it (aside from sanctimonious homilies) smacks of more than a bit of perversity."

Egon Bittner (1970)

How often do police typically use force against citizens? What kind of force is used? To get a better understanding of police use of force, let's follow Police Officer Joe Beatcop as he goes about his job and see what happens.[1]

Right after roll call, he gets a radio dispatch for family trouble. Joe and another officer arrive to find a young couple screaming at each other. The woman has a black eye and the couple's verbal sparring continues despite the arrival of the cops. Joe takes the man firmly by the arm and physically turns him away from his wife. Another officer is doing the same thing with the wife, leaving the couple back to back with each now demanding the other be arrested. After hearing the two stories, Joe has probable cause to arrest the husband and tells him to put his hands behind his back.

"I ain't going to jail!" the man retorts, and crosses his arms.

Joe's partner steps forward, making his presence obvious to the man.

"Sir, I'm asking you again. We don't want anybody to get hurt," Joe says. "Let's do this the easy way."

The man looks at Joe, measuring him up and down, then sneers at the two officers before abruptly turning and placing his hands behind his back. Under the watchful eye of his partner, Joe quickly handcuffs the man and, after searching him, takes him to the patrol car for the ride to the local jail.

But as the wife exits the house, the prisoner becomes agitated and begins to bang his head against the patrol car windows. After three smacks with his head, the guy rolls onto his back and begins to kick at the window. Joe opens the patrol car door and sprays some chemical irritant into the man's face. The man continues to scream but does cease his attempts to kick out the window.

After a few minutes the man calms down. Joe opens the car window allowing some air in the back seat and the ride to jail is uneventful.

Shortly after leaving the jail, Joe gets another run. A local business owner is calling about some teenagers hanging in front of his business. Joe pulls up, exits the car purposefully, and begins a slow walk toward the teens. The teens in turn move nonchalantly around the corner, avoiding a confrontation with Joe.

Joe gets a cup of coffee and, halfway through it, he receives a radio broadcast about a street robbery. Joe quickly responds to the area. The suspect description is vague — male Hispanic, 20-25, medium height, slight built with a green jacket. A gun was used in the offense.

Joe spots a guy fitting the description. Joe exits the police car, careful to keep the car between himself and the suspect, and points his gun at the man, ordering him to put his hands up and stand still. Other officers arrive, the man is handcuffed and searched. An officer brings the victim for a possible identification, and after carefully looking the suspect over, the victim tells the officers, "That's not the guy."

Joe explains the situation to the man, uncuffs him, and apologizes for the inconvenience. A short time later, the cops give up the search.

It's apparently one of those nights. Joe gets a radio run for a burglary alarm at a large warehouse on his beat. As other officers surround the building, Joe finds the back door unlocked. Joe and another officer then enter the building for a search. On the second floor, they find a man pulling papers from a filing cabinet. Joe points his gun at the man, demanding he kneel on the floor and keep his hands up over his head. The man complies, but begins yelling "I'm the owner!"

Another officer on the scene confirms the man is indeed the owner, who apparently entered the wrong code on his alarm panel. The owner is angry and demands to speak to Joe's supervisor as he wants to make a citizen's complaint. The whole episode annoys Joe but he decides not to let it ruin his dinner. At his favorite restaurant, while Joe is working his way through a large order of french fries, two men begin arguing loudly. The other customers look nervously in Joe's direction, waiting for him to take action. Joe turns up his police radio, hoping the two will realize they are in the presence of the law and desist, but they continue the argument at an even higher volume.

Irritated and wishing again that he'd accepted his brother-in-law's offer of a job selling aluminum siding, Joe strides across the room and bangs his nightstick loudly on the counter

The restaurant goes silent as a tomb. "What do these two owe you?" Joe asks the owner. The owner quickly gives Joe a bill which he thrusts at the two men.

"Pay it and get out!" Joe says in a voice low with menace.

"But I'm not done," one of the men whines.

Joe gives him a look that would quell a prison riot. He grabs the man's arm, lifts him to his feet and gives him a slight nudge toward the cash register.

The men quickly pay and leave. As Joe goes back to his table, the other customers begin to applaud.

Back in his patrol car, Joe is hoping that his last couple of hours will be uneventful. No such luck. There's a distraught mental patient on the town square and he's cutting himself with a knife.

When Joe gets to the square, other officers are around the man, keeping their distance, and trying to negotiate with him. A supervisor sees Joe arrive. "Get the beanbag shotgun," he orders.

Joe rushes back to his patrol car, gets the beanbag shotgun[2] out of the trunk, and sprints back to the scene. The officers have used their car lights to illuminate the man, who is now covered with blood, waving the knife and screaming at the cops "Kill me! Kill me!"

The supervisor gives the nod to Joe and he steadies himself, lining up the man's chest and fires. The beanbag round hits the man flush in the mid-section. He drops the knife and goes down. Other officers swarm around the man and quickly get him handcuffed.

The mental patient is signed in to the psychiatric ward at the local hospital, and Joe spends the last hour of his tour at the station working on a use-of-force report.

Let's review Joe's use of force. On the first family trouble, Joe uses chemical irritant (mace) on the prisoner kicking at the window. Does the fact that Joe used force on a handcuffed man raise any flags?

Not too many people would question the use of the beanbag shotgun deployed against the mental patient. But what if Joe's aim had been off and the beanbag round had struck the man in the face, a potentially fatal shot? Is our judgment on police tactics dependent on the outcome? Hit the guy in the chest — good job. Six inches higher and he dies — excessive use of force!

Twice during the hypothetical shift, Joe pointed his gun at citizens: the robbery suspect and the business owner who forgot his alarm code. Should pointing a gun at a citizen be described as police use of force? What if Joe had the gun visible in his hand, holding it at his side? How about leaving the gun in the holster but grabbing it as though he was about to pull it out? Should display of the weapon be called a use of force?

Joe displayed another weapon, his nightstick, during his interrupted meal. When he banged his stick on the counter, was that threatening force? Using force?

Several times, Joe puts his hands on people. He separates the husband and the wife, taking the man by the arm and physically moving him away from the wife. He grabs the disorderly man in the restaurant, pulls him to his feet, and gives him a slight push toward the cash register. In both these instances, Joe is clearly using physical force — his body strength — against citizens. Should Joe's police department count these as use-of-force incidents?

Lastly, in a less obvious fashion, Joe used force against the teens on the corner. His arrival in a marked police car, his presence in uniform, and the deliberate walk toward the teens, was an expression of force that resulted in moving them off the corner.

The Definitional Dilemma

Almost all citizens understand that the threat of force, and sometimes force itself, is a necessary part of police work. Jerome Skolnick and James Fyfe (1993:37), who have written extensively on police issues, note:

> As long as some members of society do not comply with law and resist the police, force will remain an inevitable part of policing. Cops, especially, understand that. Indeed, anybody who fails to understand the centrality of force to police work has no business in a police uniform.

Everyone, cops and citizens alike, recognizes that the authority to use force against citizens is an awesome responsibility. And, in principle, we all agree that police should use force only when necessary, and that officers should never use excessive force. That police departments should monitor and investigate their officers' use of force, and discipline and fire those "bad apples" who abuse citizens, is also part of the general consensus.

The dilemma is this: there is no clear agreement on what constitutes legitimate police use of force. Police around the country operate under a variety of force policies (if they exist at all), and equipment, training, and reporting protocols vary widely.

Nevertheless, there are at least points of wide agreement. No one would argue that discharging a firearm at a citizen should be described as anything but deadly force. At the other end of the spectrum, the badge, the gun, and the distinctive uniforms are symbolic of the implied force inherent in the appearance of a police officer. Yet describing mere police presence or arrival as a use of force does not seem practical either.[3]

It's not only police who struggle with this issue. Criminal justice researchers have the same difficulty. Kenneth Adams notes, "Defining excessive force in a way that makes a contribution to understanding and controlling it is not a simple matter" (Adams, 1995).

Carl Klockars, another prominent researcher, defines police use of force as "the application of physical strength for coercive purposes. It includes occasions when the use of that strength is multiplied or amplified by weapons." Klockars would, however, specifically exclude from his definition of force the use of verbal threats, pounding a nightstick on a suspect's car, or brandishing a weapon. He prefers to label these actions as "a variety of persuasion" (Klockars, 1995).

The International Association of Police Chiefs (IACP) has managed a National Police Use of Force Project since 1995. For purposes of that project, IACP defines force as: "that amount of effort required by police to compel compliance from an unwilling subject." Following from that definition, excessive force according to IACP is "the application of an amount and/or frequency of force greater than that required to compel compliance from a willing or unwilling subject" (IACP, 2001).

The Commission on Accreditation of Law Enforcement Agencies (CALEA) requires police departments seeking accreditation to have a use-of-force policy stating that "personnel will use only the force necessary to accomplish lawful objectives" (CALEA, 1999). CALEA standards do not specifically define either force or excessive force.

The Department of Justice (DOJ) Memorandum of Understanding with the Washington, DC Metropolitan Police Department provides several force-related definitions. The term "use of force" is defined as "any physical coercion used to effect, influence, or persuade an individual to comply with an order from an officer" (U.S. DOJ, 2001a). The DOJ then goes on to define "serious use of force" as:

Lethal and less-than-lethal actions by MPD officers including: (i) all firearm discharges by an MPD officer with the exception of range and training incidents and discharges at animals; (ii) all uses of force by an MPD officer resulting in a broken bone or an injury requiring hospitalization; (iii) all head strikes with an impact weapon: (iv) all uses of force by an MPD officer resulting in a loss of consciousness, or that create a substantial risk of death, serious disfigurement, disability or impairment of the functioning of any body part or organ; (v) all other uses of force by an MPD officer resulting in a death; and (vi) all incidents where a person receives a bite from an MPD canine (U.S. DOJ, 2001a, Section II, #35).

The above definition illustrates the difficulty in designing definitions for application to such a complex issue. Look for instance at (iii) in the preceding paragraph: "all head strikes with an impact weapon." Officer A swings his nightstick at citizen B's head. B manages to block the blow with his arm and, because there are no resulting injuries, that is by definition a non-serious use of force.

Across town, Officer B swings his nightstick at the upper arm of citizen A, who ducks and catches the blow in the side of the head. What began at the front end of the baton blow as a non-serious use of force escalates to serious. Here again, the outcome of the use of force (injury or not) dictates how seriously the incident is judged. In evaluating the incident, the officer's intent plays second fiddle to the outcome.

The argument over particular definitions is largely, but not entirely an academic exercise. No matter how carefully crafted, a policy is only a general guideline that is simply a starting point in evaluating a specific use-of-force incident.

Use-of-Force Data

The federal Violent Crime Control and Law Enforcement Act of 1994 required the Attorney General to "acquire data about the use of excessive force by law enforcement officers" and to "publish an annual summary of the data acquired..." (McEwen, 1996a).

In response to this mandate, several data collection efforts have been initiated. However, this effort has been hampered by several obstacles. As McEwen notes, "Systematically collecting information on use of force from the Nation's more than 17,000 law enforcement agencies is difficult given the lack of standard definitions, the variety of incident recording practices, and the sensitivity of the issue" (McEwen, 1996a).

Further complicating the issue is the lack of any substantial agreement on how to measure use of force. Should the rate be calculated as a percentage of arrests? As a rate per officer? Should it be based on the number of radio runs police officers respond to? Should it based on the crime rate? On the population of the police jurisdiction?

A 1996 U.S. Department of Justice (DOJ) study of police use of force reviewed the research to date and concluded, "police use force infrequently. The data indicate that a small percentage of police-public encounters involve force" (McEwen, 1996a).

A DOJ citizen survey in 1999 found that about 20% of Americans reported having at least one face-to-face contact with a police officer in the previous year. Among those 20% of respondents, about 1% reported that the officers had used or threatened force. This 1% finding was virtually unchanged from a similar citizen survey done in 1996 (Langan et al., 2000).

The International Association of Chiefs of Police (IACP) began building a use-of-force database in 1995. Police departments from seven states contributed data to the original effort. A review of the 1995 data found that police used force 4.19 times for every 10,000 calls-for-service. The 1999 data reported to the IACP project showed that force was used 3.61 times for every 10,000 calls for service (IACP, 2001).

Officers were most likely to use force while making arrests, and in only a small number of cases — less than 1% — did the arrested person suffer serious injury. In 2,427 force incidents reported to the IACP project in 1999-2000, just over 60% of the civilians involved were uninjured and 38% suffered minor injuries. Five deaths were reported (IACP, 2001).

The IACP data also document some change in the type of force used by police. Over the five years of the project, the use of chemical weapons (commonly referred to as mace or pepper spray) increased as a percentage of the overall force used, largely replacing hands-on or physical force. At the beginning of the project in 1995, physical force was used 13 times more often than chemical irritant. In the 1999-2000 data, the ratio of physical force to chemical irritant use had dropped to 2:1. The project also found that as use of chemical force increased, firearms use by police decreased (IACP, 2001).

As noted above, arrest situations are the likeliest place for police use of force to occur. Using a very broad definition of force, the 1996 Justice Department study reported that fewer than one of five arrests involved police use of physical force, with the majority of the force used described as low-level, mostly pushing or grabbing. About 2.1% of arrests involved use of weapons by police, with chemical irritant the most likely weapon used; and firearms were used in only 0.2% of arrests. To put that into perspective, a firearm was used by police in only two of every 10,000 arrests (McEwen, 1996a).

Between 1976 and 1998, police officers in the United States killed an average of 373 individuals each year. The highest year was 1994, when 459 individuals were killed. The lowest year was 1987, when 296 individuals were killed. The table below shows the number of people killed by police officers in the United States in selected years, as well as the rate per 100,000 population aged 13 and over.

Year	Number Killed	Rate/100,000
1976	415	.24
1980	457	.25
1985	321	.18
1990	379	.17
1995	382	.16
1998	367	.16

As the table indicates, the use of deadly force by police has steadily declined over the past two decades. From 1976 to 1998, the last year for which figures are available, the 13 and over population of the United States increased by 47 million people, and there are now approximately 200,000 more police officers employed than there were in 1976. Yet the number of people killed by the police has remained relatively constant (Brown and Langan, 2001).[4]

Discussion Questions

(1) Write out a brief definition of police use of force. What are the key elements in your definition? Should the definition of police use of force be broad or narrow?

(2) Describe an encounter you or an acquaintance has had with the police. Did force or the threat of force play a role in this encounter?

(3) You have just been appointed mayor. Write out a clear and concise policy statement on use of force for your police officers.

Notes

1. The incidents described are for illustrative purposes only. Such a string of incidents on a single shift would be unusual.

2. The "beanbag" shotgun is a less-than-lethal force alternative. It is a regular shotgun that fires a small cloth bag filled with metal pellets. It is designed to temporarily stun and incapacitate a combative person.

3. Police trainers spend a lot of time developing recruits with "command presence." The belief is those who appear competent, professional, and physically fit will gain compliance by their very appearance.

4. The number of police officers killed in the line of duty has also steadily declined over the past 25 years. From a rate of about 27 per 100,000 officers in 1976, the rate dropped to 10 per 100,000 in 1998 (Brown and Langan, 2001).

Chapter 3. Legal Boundaries

"We must never allow the theoretical, sanitized world of our imagination to replace the dangerous and complex world that policemen face every day. What constitutes 'reasonable' action may seem quite different to someone facing a possible assailant than to someone analyzing the question at leisure."

United States v. Sanchez (9th Cir. 1990)

There are two U.S. Supreme Court decisions that provide the legal framework for evaluating police use of force. The first is Tennessee v. Garner, a 1985 decision. The second is Graham v. Connor, a decision handed down in 1989. A brief review of each case follows.

Tennessee v. Garner (1985)

On October 3, 1974, just before 11:00 p.m., two Memphis police officers received a radio dispatch for a prowler. When they arrived at the address, Officers Elton Hymon and Leslie Wright were met by a woman who advised them she had heard breaking glass and believed someone was in the house next door. Officer Hymon started toward the rear of the house. Just as he arrived at the back edge of the house, he heard a door slam and saw someone run away from him across the back yard.

There was a chain-link fence across the back yard. The fleeing suspect stopped at the fence momentarily. Officer Hymon shone his flashlight on the suspect and was able to see the suspect's face and hands. Hymon did not see any weapon, and later testified that he was "reasonably sure" that the suspect was not armed. Hymon described the suspect as 17 or 18 years old and about 5'5" to 5'7" tall.

The suspect crouched at the base of the fence. Officer Hymon yelled out "Police, halt!" The suspect began climbing the fence. Hymon, believing that if the suspect got over the fence, he would get away, fired one shot at the suspect. The bullet hit the suspect in the head, killing him.

The suspect was identified as Edward Garner, a 15-year-old Memphis eighth-grader. Garner had ransacked one room of the house, scattering the owner's belongings around the room. The owner later determined that $10 and a ring were missing. Ten dollars was found on Garner's body, but the ring was never recovered.

The use of deadly force by Officer Hymon in this instance was allowable under a Tennessee statute that read: "if, after notice of the intention to arrest the defendant, he either flees or forcibly resists, the officer may use all the necessary means to effect the arrest."

The Memphis Police use-of-force policy was more restrictive than the state law, but did allow use of deadly force to prevent the escape of burglary suspects.

The facts of the Garner case were reviewed by both a Memphis grand jury and the Memphis Police Firearms Review Board. Neither body took any action against Officer Hymon.

Garner's father filed suit in the U.S. District Court alleging that Hymon's use of deadly force represented a number of constitutional violations. In addition to Officer Hymon, the Memphis Police Department and the City of Memphis were named as parties to the suit.

Eleven years after Garner's death, the case made its way to the Supreme Court of the United States. In Tennessee v. Garner (1985), the Supreme Court set both a new standard for judging police deadly-force incidents and specific guidance for when police could use deadly force.

In Garner, the court's basic rationale was that deadly force by the police in essence constituted a seizure. The court declared that apprehension by deadly force is a seizure subject to the Fourth Amendment's "reasonableness" requirement. Thus, deadly-force incidents should be judged under the Fourth Amendment[1] standard prohibiting "unreasonable" seizures.

Much of the argument before the court in Garner considered whether police had the right to use deadly force against fleeing suspects including burglars such as Garner. The court agreed that while burglary is a serious crime, that fact alone did not justify the use of deadly force. Further, specifically in the case of Garner, Officer Hymon did not perceive any danger to himself from Garner. Hymon testified that he shot Garner only to prevent his escape. The court reasoned that while Officer Hymon clearly had probable cause to seize (arrest) Garner, it was unreasonable to use deadly force to effect the arrest.

In summary, the Supreme Court decision in Garner made clear two important points:

- First, use of deadly force by police was to be judged by the Fourth Amendment standard of "objectively reasonable."

- Second, the use of deadly force simply to apprehend or seize fleeing felons was on its face constitutionally unreasonable. The court specifically stated that an officer may use deadly force only if "he has probable cause to believe that the suspect poses a threat of serious physical harm, either to the officer or to others."

Note that Garner dealt only with deadly-force situations. Four years later, in Graham v. Conner, the Supreme Court made it clear that all claims of excessive police force should be judged against the Fourth Amendment "reasonableness" standard.

Graham v. Connor (1989)

Dethorne Graham was a diabetic. On the evening of November 12, 1984, Graham felt the onset of an insulin reaction. He asked a friend of his, William Berry, to drive him to a nearby convenience store so he could buy some orange juice to counteract the insulin reaction.

Graham entered the convenience store to buy the juice. However, the check-out lines were long, so Graham hurriedly left the store, jumped in the car with Berry and instructed him to drive to a friend's house instead.

Graham's quick exit from the store without making a purchase was observed by Charlotte, North Carolina Police Officer M.S. Connor. Connor followed the car driven by Berry for about one-half mile and then made a traffic stop.

Berry told Officer Connor that Graham was suffering from a "sugar reaction." Connor instructed Berry and Graham to remain in the car. Connor called for backup and also asked that another officer check with the employees of the convenience store to ensure nothing had happened.

As Connor returned to the patrol car, Graham exited Berry's car, ran around it twice, sat down on the curb, then briefly passed out.

Other Charlotte officers arrived. One of them rolled Graham over on the sidewalk and cuffed his hands behind his back, ignoring Berry's pleas to get his friend some sugar. Another officer stated: "I've seen a lot of people with sugar diabetes that never acted like this. Ain't nothing wrong with the M.F. but drunk. Lock the S.B. up."

Officers then picked up Graham and placed him face down on the hood of Berry's car. Graham regained consciousness and asked that the officers check his wallet for a diabetic card he carried. An officer told Graham to "shut up."

A friend of Graham's showed up at the scene with some orange juice, but officers refused to let him have it. Finally, Officer Connor was notified that Graham had done nothing wrong in the convenience store. Officers then drove Graham home and released him.

During his encounter with the Charlotte police Graham suffered a broken foot, cuts on his wrists, a bruised forehead, and an injured shoulder. He also claimed an injury that caused a chronic loud ringing in his right ear.

Graham sued the officers for excessive force. The case took four years to get to the U.S. Supreme Court and, in May of 1989, the court issued its ruling.

First, the court ruled that the same Fourth Amendment standard of "reasonableness" which they had relied on in Garner would be used in Graham. The court said: "Today we make explicit what was implicit in Garner's analysis, and hold that all claims that law enforcement officers have used excessive force — deadly or not — in the course of an arrest, investigatory stop, or other 'seizure' of a free citizen should be analyzed under the Fourth Amendment and its 'reasonableness' standard."[2]

The court then expounded on the concept of "reasonableness." The court first noted that the police right to arrest or to stop a person on an investigatory basis carries with it the right to use the threat of physical coercion or physical coercion itself. Further, the court said "the test of reasonableness under the Fourth Amendment is not capable of precise definition or mechanical application."

In Graham v. Connor (1989), the court identified four factors to apply to each case to determine whether or not a particular use of force is reasonable. The four factors were: the severity of the crime at issue; whether the suspect poses an immediate threat to the safety of the officers or others; whether he is actively resisting; and whether he is attempting to evade arrest by flight. The court noted that the question is "whether the totality of the circumstances justifies a particular sort of ...seizure."

Last, but probably the most important point made by the court in Graham, was that police officers are entitled to a substantial degree of latitude in making use-of-force judgments. Specifically, the court said "The 'reasonableness' of a particular use of force must be judged from the *perspective of a reasonable officer on the scene,*[3] and its calculus must embody an allowance for the fact that police officers are often forced to make split-second decisions about the amount of force necessary in a particular situation."

Together, Tennessee v. Garner and Graham v. Connor constitute the legal context for judging police use of force. In summary, the key elements in the two decisions are:

- Deadly force may not be used unless the officer has probable cause to believe the suspect poses a significant threat of death or serious physical harm to the officer or others.

- Use of force, including deadly-force decisions, should be judged under the Fourth Amendment "reasonableness" standard.

- The "reasonableness" standard is not subject to precise definition or mechanical application.

- Each situation must be viewed from the point of view of a reasonable officer on the scene, accounting for the totality of circumstances.

- Reasonableness must account for the fact that police officers make use-of-force decisions "in circumstances that are tense, uncertain, and rapidly evolving."

In judging the reasonableness of force decisions, courts may look at four factors. The four factors are the severity of the crime at issue, whether the suspect poses an immediate threat to the safety of the officers or others, whether he is actively resisting, and whether he is attempting to evade arrest by flight.

Recent Cases

In the years since these two decisions, the federal courts have ruled in a number of other cases that clarify some of the key issues in Garner and Graham.

Some appeals court cases have expanded on the concept of the immediacy of the situation and the necessity for the officer to make a split second decision.[4] For example, Schultz v. Long (1995) and Scott v. Henrich (1994) are two similar cases. Schultz attacked an officer with a hatchet and was shot dead. In Scott, officers shot and killed a man who pointed a gun at them from his front door as they were approaching his residence. Plaintiffs' lawyers in both cases argued the officers should have used other tactical options and that their failure to do so constituted excessive force. In Scott v. Henrich, the federal appeals court noted: "as long as the police use of deadly force was reasonable, the constitution does not require them to use less intrusive alternatives."

Plakas v. Drinski (1994) is perhaps the best example of the federal appellate courts' view of whether the failure of officers to utilize less lethal force options or tactics can be construed as excessive force. On February 2, 1991, in Newton County, Indiana deputies found Konstantino Plakas walking along a state road at about 9:30 p.m. Sergeant Buddy King stopped Plakas, believing he was the driver of vehicle that had run off the road about a mile away. Plakas admitted being the driver of the car and agreed to go with Sergeant King back to the vehicle. Sergeant King knew there were paramedics at the scene and Plakas may have needed treatment. The sergeant also believed Plakas was intoxicated.

Back at the vehicle, Plakas refused medical help and signed a waiver to that effect. The deputies decided to take Plakas back to the station to test him for drunkenness. Corporal Dave Koby then frisked Plakas, handcuffed him behind the back, and placed him in the rear of the patrol car for the trip to the station. Plakas complained about the handcuffing, stating he had burn scars on his chest and that the handcuffing would cause his chest to bleed. Koby told Plakas it was department policy to handcuff prisoners in that fashion and began the trip to the sheriff's office.

As Koby began to drive away, Plakas managed to open the rear door of the police car, rolled out of the car and fled into the woods. Koby radioed the escape and requested assistance. Plakas ran to the residence of Roy and Judy Ailes, a family he knew well as Plakas was engaged to the Ailes' daughter. Roy Ailes told Plakas he should surrender to the police and Plakas agreed that Ailes should go talk to the officers. Ailes found the deputies nearby, and directed them to his residence. Plakas was inside the house and when he saw the officers enter he became combative. The officers saw Plakas push his legs through the circle of his arms, thus bringing his cuffed hands to the front of his body. Plakas then picked up a fireplace poker and swung it at Sergeant Koby, injuring Koby's wrist. Plakas, still carrying the poker, then fled from the house. Deputy Jeff Drisinski, who had responded to assist, saw Plakas flee the house and chased after him.

Drinski and another deputy eventually cornered Plakas in a clearing in the woods. For 15 to 30 minutes, Drinski tried to persuade Plakas to drop the poker and surrender. During the negotiation, Plakas repeatedly stated that Drinski would have to shoot him stating, "My life isn't worth anything." Finally, from about 12 to 15 feet away, Plakas raised the poker and charged Drinski. Drinski tried to retreat but backed into a tree, and with Plakas now only feet away, Drinski fired his weapon once, striking Plakas in the chest and killing him.

Plakas's estate sued Drinski and the Newton County Sheriff's office. The plaintiff argued that Drinski had a duty to use alternative methods short of deadly force to resolve the situation. The claim against the county rested on the proposition that Drinski should have been equipped and trained to use alternative methods. Plakas specifically suggested that chemical spray or a police dog could have been used to disarm Plakas.

The federal appellate court rejected these arguments, noting, "we recognize that the decision to shoot can only be made after the briefest reflection, so brief that 'reflection' is the wrong word. As Plakas moved toward Drinski, was he supposed to think of an attack dog, of Perra's [another officer at the scene] CS gas, of how fast he could run backwards? Our answer is, and has been no because there is too little time for the officer to do so and too much opportunity to second-guess that officer" (Plakas v. Drinski, 1994).

The rulings in these three cases affirmed the principle that deadly-force incidents must be judged from the precise moment the "seizure," i.e. deadly force, occurs. In Plakas, the court wrote, "We do not return to the prior segments of the event and, in light of hindsight, reconsider whether the prior police decisions were correct."

Tennessee v. Garner (1985) established the principle that a police officer could use deadly force when faced with a significant threat of serious injury or death to himself or others. Where officers are directly threatened with a weapon, the principle is relatively easy to apply. But how much latitude should officers be given in making decisions where the threat is less certain?

Anderson v. Russell (2001) is a case that directly addresses the issue. On December 28, 1991, Police Officer David Russell was working an off-duty security detail at a shopping mall in Prince George's County, Maryland. A patron approached Russell and pointed to a man named Maurice Anderson, advising the officer he believed a visible bulge under Anderson's clothing might have been a gun. Anderson was wearing several layers of clothes as well as a wool hat pulled down over his head.

Russell spent the next several minutes following Anderson around the mall and observed the bulge under Anderson's sweater, which he believed might have been a gun. Russell and his partner, Officer David Pearson, decided not to confront Anderson until he left the mall. They followed Anderson to the parking lot and, with guns drawn, ordered him to raise his hands and get down on his knees. Anderson initially raised his hands, but a moment later lowered his hand, reaching toward the bulge. Russell fired his gun, striking Anderson in the leg and causing permanent damage.

Anderson did not have a gun. The bulge was a radio and Anderson was wearing headphones hidden under his hat. His movement to the "bulge" was an attempt to turn down his radio. The court noted that Russell's mistake had "tragic consequences to Anderson," yet in ruling for Russell the court said: "Officers need not be absolutely sure... of the nature of the threat or the suspect's intent to cause them harm — the Constitution does not require that certitude precede the act of self protection" (Anderson v. Russell, 2001).

Certainly, reasonable officers may disagree about the constitutional "reasonableness" of police action in various cases. Thus, in expounding on the notion put forth in the Graham case that "objective reasonableness" is not subject to precise definition, the court in Malley v. Briggs (1986) said: "The objective reasonableness test is met if 'officers of reasonable competence could disagree on the legality of the defendant's action.'"

Are officers ever justified in using deadly force against a suspect who is running away? In Garner, the court stated that if the officer has probable cause to believe the person poses a serious threat of injury or death to officers or others, it is not constitution-ally unreasonable to use deadly force to stop that person's escape.

Garner clearly allows police officers to use force to protect themselves and others from threats to their safety. However, as Special Agent John Hall, a legal instructor at the FBI Academy notes: "What is often disputed is an officer's assessment of a threat and the level of force selected to counter it. As a general principle, the level of force used should be tailored to the nature of the threat that prompted its use. The Fourth Amendment does not require that officers choose the least intrusive level of force, only a reasonable one" (Hall, 1992).

The legal principles embodied by Tennessee v. Garner and Graham v. Connor are logical and relatively easy to articulate. What is more difficult is applying these principles to the complex situations faced by police officers.

Discussion Questions

(1) Choose a well-known use-of-deadly-force incident. Try to apply the standards under Garner and Graham to the incident.

(2) The courts have ruled that use-of-force incidents are to be judged from the point of view of a "reasonable offi-cer on the scene." What impact does this legal standard have on action by citizen police review boards?

(3) Can police departments set use-of-force policies and standards that differ from the legal standard? If so, should they?

Notes

1. The Fourth Amendment to the U.S. Constitution reads — "The right of the people to be secure in their persons, houses, papers, and effects, against unreasonable searches and seizures, shall not be violated, and no Warrants shall issue, but upon probable cause, supported by Oath or af-

firmation, and particularly describing the place to be searched, and the persons or things to be seized."

2. Use of force in custodial situations would usually be judged under an Eighth Amendment standard.

3. Emphasis added by the author.

4. The 94 U.S. judicial districts are organized into 12 regional circuits, each of which has a court of appeals. A court of appeals hears appeals from the district courts located within its circuit. Federal circuit courts are the courts directly below the Supreme Court. Their decisions are binding only within their geographic boundaries.

Chapter 4. The Race Divide

*"When the police chief is called at 3:30 in the morning
and told 'Chief, one of our cops has just shot a kid,' the
chief's first questions are: 'What color is the cop?
What color is the kid?'*

*"And, the reporter asked, if the answer is, 'The cop is
white, the kid is black?' 'He gets dressed,' replied
Bouza.*

> Former Minneapolis Police Chief
> Anthony Bouza (quoted in Geller and
> Scott, 1992).

Nowhere is the racial divide in America quite as deep as in
the sometimes antagonistic relationship between minorities, particularly African Americans, and the police. The history of police
racism, from police-sanctioned violence against blacks to neglect
of crime problems in black communities, is one of the most
shameful chapters in American police history. Police, after all,
were the enforcers of Jim Crow laws. Police officers in the north
and south were prominent in sometimes brutally breaking up the
civil rights marches of the 1960s, and police officers arrested Rosa
Parks for refusing to give up her bus seat to a white man. Most of
the civil disorder of the last century stemmed from confrontations
between police and African-American citizens.

While other minority groups have complaints about discriminatory policing, the issue is most vivid for African Americans. As
Randall Kennedy notes, the primary racial conflict emanating
from the criminal justice system is what he describes as the:

> ...white-black confrontation. This is the conflict that has served as
> the great object lesson for American law, the conflict that has
> given birth to much of the federal constitutional law of criminal
> procedure, and the conflict that remains the pervasive and volatile

point of racial friction within federal and state courthouses. ...More than any other racial divide in America, however, it is the racial frontier separating whites from blacks where the difficulties have proven hardest to overcome (Kennedy, 1997, p.xii).

The relationships among crime, race, and police behavior are complex. Is the behavior of police officers — from stop-and-frisk practices, to traffic stops, to the use of force — influenced by racial factors?

In summarizing the research on deadly force by police, Locke (1995:140) notes: "What every single study of police use of *fatal* force has found is that persons of color (principally black males) are a disproportionately high number of the persons shot by police compared to their representation in the general population. Where the studies diverge are the reasons for such disproportionality." A review by Binder and Fridell (1984) concluded that any findings of racial discrimination in police shootings were confounded by variables that supported alternative explanations. A more recent study of police shootings in 170 large U.S. cities found that *both* racial inequality and a city's violent crime rates were causal factors in police killings of African Americans (Jacobs and O'Brien, 1998).

Whatever the cause or causes of the racial disparities in police shootings, the racial gap is narrowing. Studies from the 1960s and 70s found African Americans fatally shot by the police at a rate six times that of whites. By the late 1980s, that disparity had been cut in half (Walker, 2000). Some researchers believe the current disparate rates of shootings mirror "involvement in serious crime rather than systematic discrimination" (Walker, 2000). While research is inconclusive, the concerns about discriminatory policing, particularly related to African Americans, remain a major source of racial tension in the country. Perhaps no other issue expresses this tension more clearly than racial profiling.

The Racial Profiling Issue

Nowhere is the debate on the role of race in policing more intense than in the ongoing national discussion on racial profiling.

Discussion on the issue captures the stark differences between many in the police community and the view of many African Americans. Confronted with accusations of profiling, police respond with statistics on crime in black communities. They suggest that racial differences in traffic stops, arrests, and use of force stem not from discriminatory policing but from higher rates of crime among African Americans. For some police officials, there is a common sense connection between higher rates of traffic stops for blacks, as an example, and good policing. Harris (1999:269) notes that police "...may engage in these practices for a simple reason: they help catch criminals. Since blacks represent a disproportionate share of those arrested for certain crimes, police believe that it makes sense to stop a disproportionate share of blacks."

Maryland State Police Lieutenant Ernest Leatherbury expressed this point of view succinctly, stating: "...stopping an outsized number of blacks was not racism, but rather 'an unfortunate byproduct of sound police practices'" (ibid., p.268).

The issue of racial profiling originated in the police practice of using "profiles" to identify suspected drug couriers in airports and on the highways. Some of the early training in profiling, largely provided by the federal Drug Enforcement Administration, made use of race or ethnicity as a marker for identifying possible couriers. One document, used for training of New Jersey state police, "teaches troopers to zero in on minorities when scanning state roadways for possible drug traffickers. Titled *Occupant Identifiers for a Possible Drug Courier*, the document instructs troopers to look out for 'Colombian males, Hispanic males, Hispanic and a black male together, Hispanic male and female posing as a couple'" (Kocieniewski and Hanley, 2000).

The issue gained national attention after a controversial police shooting on the New Jersey Turnpike in April of 1998 that some labeled an example of racial profiling. In court, the troopers involved in the shooting acknowledged they stopped the vehicle involved because its occupants were black. "The troopers said their supervisors had trained them to focus on black- and brown-skinned drivers because, they were told, they were more likely to be drug traffickers" (Common Sense..., 2002).

New Jersey Governor Christie Whitman subsequently conceded that New Jersey state troopers were practicing racial profiling. In 1999, New Jersey entered into a consent decree with the U.S. Department of Justice promising reforms to end the practice. (The consent decree is available at www.state.nj.us./lps/corcaid.pdf.)

Racial profiling has since become a broad term denoting racially-biased policing. There has been much debate on exactly when and how police should "profile," as well as exactly what constitutes "racial profiling." A widely accepted definition is the one devised by Northeastern University Law Professor Deborah Ramirez, who defines police racial profiling as "any police-initiated action that relies on the race, ethnicity or national origin of an individual rather than the behavior of an individual or information that leads the police to a particular individual who has been identified as being, or having been, engaged in criminal activity" (Erford and Zeman, 2001).

The practice of profiling as defined above will find few supporters. A number of state and municipalities have passed legislation prohibiting the practice of racial profiling, and polls indicate that the overwhelming majority of Americans are against the practice. Yet, most of the policy discussion to date has assumed that racial profiling is a common practice. Publicity surrounding New Jersey state troopers and profiling, together with some early research in both New Jersey and Maryland, painted a picture of American policing steeped in racism. For example, John Lamberth, a Temple University psychology professor who did studies comparing rates of stops and arrests between black and white drivers in the late 1980s and early 1990s stated in court testimony:

> Absent some other explanation for the dramatically disproportionate number of stops of blacks, it would appear that the race of the occupants and/or drivers of the cars is a decisive factor or a factor with great explanatory power. I can say to a reasonable degree of statistical probability that the disparity outlined here is strongly consistent with the existence of a discriminatory policy, official or de facto, of targeting blacks for stops and investigation... (Lamberth, 1996).

Lamberth's conclusions were echoed in public opinion polls. A number of polls conducted in the late 1990s found widespread belief among both blacks and whites that police racism directed at African Americans was common. Multiple studies found a majority of white citizens agreeing with the proposition that police were "far more likely to harass and discriminate against blacks than whites" (Harris, 1999).

More recent studies have thrown that conventional wisdom into doubt. While a summary of five studies on racial profiling by the U.S. General Accounting Office (U.S. GAO, 2000) found African-American motorists more likely to be stopped by police than whites, a U.S. Department of Justice (DOJ) study of 19.3 million police stops in 1999 found no concrete evidence of racial profiling. The DOJ study found that the group most likely to be stopped by the police was white males between 16 and 24 years of age. The DOJ study did find that black drivers were more likely to be searched than white drivers, but complaints of excessive force against the police fell equally among all racial and ethnic groups ("DOJ Data...," 2002). And a recent study by the U.S. Bureau of Justice Statistics found that "African-Americans are actually less likely to be subject to police-initiated stops than are white Americans" (Walker, 2000).

But the evidence on racial profiling continues to be mixed. For example, a 1999 study in New York looked at racial patterns in the stop-and-frisk[1] practices of the New York City Police Department. Researchers found that both blacks and Hispanics were stopped in numbers higher than would be expected based on population. African Americans, for instance, constituted 25.6% of New York's population, but accounted for 50.6% of all those stopped. The study also reviewed the legal basis for the stops and found minorities no more likely to be detained without "reasonable suspicion" than whites, but when cases involving physical force were separated, racial disparities were found (New York State Attorney General's..., 1999).

Summary

Review of the research does not provide clear answers to the extent of bias in American policing. It is clear that African-American citizens are more likely to experience police force used against them than other ethnic groups are. Yet the factors underlying this finding are complex. The crime rates in urban areas with a high concentration of African Americans are notably high. These areas are also plagued by high poverty rates, high rates of joblessness, drug addiction, poor educational opportunities and a variety of other social problems that make them fertile ground for community disorder and crime. Efforts to attribute use of force against minorities simply to biased policing sometimes ignore the community context in which police officers work. Yet those who claim policing is free of bias too often gloss over the legacy of police discrimination and the all-too-prevalent biases that affect each and every one of us as human beings. The challenge for police and community leaders is to implement policies and systems that mitigate and control bias as a factor in police interactions with citizens.

Beyond Statistics

For black Americans, profiling is more than an issue of statistics. The issue is one that is felt very personally. Henry Louis Gates (1997:151-152) captured the essence of the personal nature of profiling in a piece in the *New Yorker* magazine:

> Blacks — in particular, black men—swap their experiences of police encounters like war stories, and there are few who don't have more than one story to tell. Erroll McDonald, one of the few prominent blacks in publishing, tells of renting a Jaguar in New Orleans and being stopped by the police — simply "to show cause why I shouldn't be deemed a problematic Negro in a possible stolen car." Wynton Marsalis says, "Shit, the police slapped me upside the head when I was in high school. I wasn't Wynton Marsalis then. I was just another nigger standing out somewhere on the street whose head could be slapped and did get slapped." The crime novelist Walter Mosley recalls, "When I was a kid in Los

Angeles, they use to spot me all the time, beat on me, follow me around, tell me that I was stealing things." Nor does William Julius Wilson wonder why he was stopped near a small New England town by a policeman who wanted to know what he was doing in those parts. There's a moving violation that many Americans-Americans know as D.W.B.: Driving While Black.

David Harris, an Ohio attorney who has researched and written on racial profiling, notes: "It is virtually impossible to find black people who do not feel that they have experienced racial profiling. These experiences have a deep psychological and emotional impact on the individuals involved, and they also have a significant connection to many of the most basic problems in criminal justice and race" (Harris, 1999:269).

The notion that racial profiling is non-existent would be laughingly dismissed by most African Americans. Whites and blacks experiencing the same police behavior will describe their experiences much differently. A white citizen stopped for a traffic violation is unlikely to attribute any racial motivation to the stop regardless of the race of the officer. Yet, when asked the first thing that pops into their mind on being stopped by the police, black recruits in police academy classes that I teach answer unanimously, "Profiling!"

History, as much as current practice, likely colors the interaction between African-American citizens and police. In describing the animosity between police and black communities during the 1960s, Kennedy (1997:115) noted the oft-stated belief that the police acted more like a repressive force rather than public servants working to protect and serve: "Fueling this perception, substantially supported in fact, that at least in part for racial reasons police tended to behave in a distinctively rude, overbearing, contemptuous fashion in predominantly black neighborhoods, a manner that gave credence to the notion that, in black communities, police constituted an occupying force rather than a cadre of useful civil servants."

It is reasonable to ask if vestiges of that attitude are still present in too many police interactions, particularly with African Americans. Even an avid supporter of the police, such as writer

Heather MacDonald (1999:37) notes, "Too many officers have a rude, contemptuous attitude."

The higher rate of street crime-related behavior by African Americans is not a figment of racist imagination. Complex reasons underlie that reality. As Kennedy (1997:74) notes: "Given the deprivations blacks have faced, it should come as no surprise that, relative to their proportion of the population, blacks are more likely than whites to commit street crimes. That is a reality that is indifferent to the embarrassment of those ashamed of the criminality that poor economic, social, cultural, and moral conditions spawn."

That is also a reality that is going to affect police officer behavior, as well as the behavior of citizens, both black and white. Even a fervent advocate for the betterment of black Americans like Reverend Jesse Jackson is affected by this reality. "There is nothing more painful for me at this stage in my life than to walk down the street and hear footsteps and start to think about robbery and then look around and see it's somebody white and feel relieved," Jackson said in 1994 (ibid.).

The racial divide in America has been particularly resistant to easy solutions. Racial tensions remain part of the American landscape, in business, government, and civic life. Policing is where these tensions are most acute, and our progress in improving race relations will depend a great deal on ensuring that the police officers work with respect for the residents in the communities they serve.

Discussion Questions

(1) To what extent do you believe police practice racial profiling?

(2) What steps would you suggest to government officials to reduce tensions after a racially-charged police incident?

(3) Do you agree with the proposition that tension between police and the community mirrors racial tensions in other areas of community life?

(4) How would you rate your local police department's community relations? What improvements would you suggest?

Notes

1. "Stop and Frisk" refers to the police practice of briefly detaining individuals based on reasonable suspicion that the individual may be involved in criminal activity.

Chapter 5. Force Options

"He had shaggy hair and looked as if he hadn't shaved that morning. His shirt was wrinkled and his clip-on tie was pinned off to one side of his collar, a pet peeve of mine. His gun belt, which had originally been black but was now brown from wear, hung from him like he was Mister Goodwrench, and his hat was hanging from his holster."

William Bratton (1998)

The three drug runners just got careless. They did not want to draw attention to themselves, headed to Detroit with a trunk full of drugs and the three of them heavily armed. But at three o'clock in the morning and I-75 pretty well deserted, the driver let his foot get a little heavy. Now, a Cincinnati cop was behind them, lights and siren going.

As they pulled over, an animated discussion began. "Be cool!" the passenger advised. "Just a speeding ticket."

"I ain't got no license, man! They're going to see the guns." The driver pulled the gun from his waistband and reaching down, shoved it under the seat.

The dealer in the backseat was calmer. He had spent much of his life in prison and was experienced in dealing with cops. He also knew if the cops found the drugs or the guns, he would be sitting in the penitentiary for a lot of years. He picked up his Tec-9 from the floor and racked a round into the chamber. The loud click silenced the other two. "Ain't going back to jail," he told them. "There's three of us and we got more shit." He tapped the gun barrel on the seat. "Let's do it."

The officer began to approach, but hesitated at the rear of the dealer's car. The movement by the driver had made the officer wary. His hand was resting on his gun. "Sir," he called to the driver, "get out of the car and come back here for me."

The driver looked back, squinting into the lights from the cop car. "Just wait," he told the others and stepped out of the car. He saw there were two cops. He walked back toward the officers, holding his hands in the air. "Hey, no problem."

"Do you have a license?" the officer asked.

"No, I lost it."

"No big deal. Maybe one of your friends has a license."

"Yeah. The guy in the front seat, Bobby. I think he has one. I was just driving cause he got sleepy."

A third officer materialized behind him, taking him firmly by the arm.

"We're going to handcuff you for a few minutes," the cop said. "Just till we get this straightened out. No big deal." The handcuffs were on him before he could reply.

Now one of the officers called to the passenger. "Bobby, could you step back here for me."

Bobby shoved open the car door. "Chill," he hissed. "They got nothin." Bobby stepped out of the car, quickly checking the 9MM tucked under his shirt, touching it, then raising his hands. "What's up, officer? We're in kind of a hurry."

"We got a slight problem," the cop said. "Your buddy doesn't have a driver's license. But he says you have one. Could I see it?"

Moving slowly, Bobby produced his license and handed it to one of the cops. The cop took it and moved slightly away, talking into his radio.

"No problem," Bobby repeated to himself as they waited. A minute later, the cop stepped back, and, as a team, the two cops each had him by the arms, pulling them back and putting handcuffs on him. "You've got a warrant on you, Bobby," the cop explained, "No big deal. We'll try to work it out."

An officer was frisking him as he spoke, and a second later pulled the gun from Bobby's waistband. "This is a problem," the officer said. "What's the guy's name in the back seat?"

"It's Jerome."

"Is he carrying?"

Bobby pretended like he hadn't heard.

"OK," the cop said. They put Bobby in another patrol car.

Jerome was watching out the back window. The Tec-9 was heavy in his lap. The spotlights from the patrol car kept him from seeing anything. Suddenly, a voice boomed from the cop car speaker.

"Jerome. We know you've got a gun. Leave it in the back seat and step out of the car with your hands up."

Jerome banged the seat in frustration. He couldn't even see the cops. They must be behind the cars. He waited, holding the gun, weighing his options, before throwing the gun on the floor and stepping out of the car.

A couple of hours later, with the paperwork completed, I had Jerome in my patrol car, taking him to jail. During the ride, he'd told his story, a life alternating between jail and time on the streets selling drugs. We also talked about the traffic stop and the way the arrest of Jerome and his friends had gone down. There was something I had been wanting to ask him all night.

"Why didn't you do it?" I asked. "When we first got you stopped, you had us outnumbered and outgunned. We didn't even know what was going on."

Jerome considered it. "We thought about it," he admitted. "I was ready at the start. But I guess you guys just looked too good." He laughed at himself. "Ain't that a bitch." And I had to laugh with him.

The situation could have gone bad in a big hurry. After talking with Jerome, I was convinced that the traffic stop could easily have ended in a shootout, with cops and suspects dead. But the cops on the scene had acted in a fashion that prevented violence from erupting. When Jerome stated, "you guys just looked too good," what did he mean?

For me, it was confirmation that professionalism, a competence demonstrated through purposeful verbal communications and careful tactics, had in fact forestalled the need for deadly force.

When a police officer arrives on the scene, everyone there begins to take his measure. His physical presence, his verbalizations, the things he says and does in that first few seconds can dramatically alter the dynamics of the situation. The officer's reading of the situation and his response can defuse the potential for violence or in some cases, act as a spark in an explosive atmosphere.

In use-of-force situations, police officers have multiple options. Making the right choices at the right time is the art of policing.

Force Options — *Officer Presence*

Discussion of police force options begins with the physical presence of a police officer. Consider Officer Smith — overweight, stomach hanging over the gunbelt, hat askew, smoking a cigar, and last night's chili dinner still on his shirt. Contrast this with Officer Jones — fit, uniform neatly pressed, shoes shined, erect posture.

Jones is the picture of competence and professionalism. Smith personifies the stereotype of the overweight, lazy cop. Smith may, in fact, be a competent officer. But he has to overcome the impression that his appearance communicates.

The importance of a commanding presence has been recognized since the beginning of modern policing. The distinctive tall hats of the original English Bobbies in London were issued to help create an imposing presence.

In a more recent variation, former chief William Bratton (now head of the Los Angeles Police Department) describes the reaction after he successfully fought to have the New York City Transit Police upgrade their firearms from .38 revolvers to the Glock 9mm Semi-Auto Pistols. "I was with Cal Mathis, out in uniform on one of my ride-alongs one night, when a couple of kids no more than thirteen years old eyeballed us. 'Hey, man,' one said as we walked by, 'you guys got Glocks!' These kids knew the firearms just by looking at them. It became a big thing on the platforms, 'Hey, Transit's got nines!'" (Bratton, 1998).

Force Options — *Verbal Communications/ Commands*

Most police officers recognize that good verbal skills are crucial to their job. Human communications are difficult under the best of circumstances. In situations where emotions are high, while stress levels for both officers and civilians are soaring, communicating effectively becomes an extraordinary challenge.

Police are expected to listen empathically to victims, react calmly when verbally abused, be respectful and polite in all dealings with others, be persuasive with people they are arresting, and provide clear and direct commands in an emergency. In short, good cops need the communications skills of a therapist combined with the command voice and presence of a drill instructor.

Force Options — *Multiple Officers*

Some situations call for multiple officers. A suspect ready to fight one police officer may comply when confronted with two or three cops. Police agencies typically recognize that certain situations are high risk — robbery and domestic violence calls are two examples. In these high-risk situations, dispatchers will automatically send multiple officers. Multiple officers enhance the "police presence" effect and represent a higher level of force than a single officer.

Force Options — *Chemical Irritant (CI)*

Chemical irritant (CI), more commonly known as mace, has become an increasingly popular force option for police departments. According to the figures provided by participating police agencies to the International Chiefs of Police (IACP) Use of Force project, in 1995 police used physical force about 13 times for each use of chemical irritant. Yet, by 2000, this ratio had dropped to 2 to 1. The project further documented that as use of CI increased, firearms use decreased. In fact, by 2000, the police use of CI was greater than the combined totals for electronic weapons, impact weapons, and firearms combined (IACP, 2001).

There are three main types of CI: OC, more commonly known as pepper spray, CN gas, and CS gas. CN and CS are variations of tear gas. All three work in much the same fashion. They cause severe burning of the eyes and mucus membranes, and restrict breathing. In the majority of cases, the person sprayed is incapacitated, allowing officers to control and handcuff the person without further force. A U.S. Department of Justice (DOJ) study found that 90% of suspects sprayed with OC by Baltimore County Police Officers were incapacitated (Edwards et al., 1997). This same study found that use of the OC spray reduced officer injuries, suspect injuries, and assaults on police officers.

CI products vary widely, not only by chemical composition, but in strength as measured by the percentage of active ingredients in the spray. A review of various CI products by the U.S. National of Justice (1994) concluded that police agencies should consider "product's formulation, concentration level, range, type of trigger mechanism, spray pattern, and presence or absence of a safety mechanism."

By any measure, CI is a valuable force option with several striking advantages. It's easy to use, it allows officers to maintain distance from the person being sprayed, its physical effects are temporary and minor, and it works most of the time. Given this, it's not surprising that CI is an increasingly popular option for officers.

Force Options — *"Hands-on" or Physical Control*

Policing is a hands-on business. Officers are constantly separating people, restraining them with body weight, using escort holds to move them from place to place, and sometimes striking them. Skolnick and Fyfe quote an active city officer: "I can't think of a single day when I didn't put my hands on somebody" (Skolnick and Fyfe, 1993:116).

The most frequent type of physical force used by police officers consists of low-level actions, such as pushing and grabbing

(McEwen, 1996a). Less frequently, officers may strike with a hand or forearm, kick, throw to the ground, or wrestle with a person. Some police training includes pressure points, wristlocks or arm holds, neck restraints, and choke holds as physical control techniques. These techniques range from pain compliance methods like pressure points, to attempts to cause injury (kicks or blows at joints), to deadly-force response (chokeholds).

Success in using physical control is contingent on officer skills, training, and physical conditioning. The vast majority of police officers are not Steven Seagal type martial-arts experts, and their odds of success in a physical confrontation with a suspect who is likely to be younger, stronger, and under the influence of drugs is questionable at best.

Probably the biggest deterrent to officers becoming involved in physical fights with suspects is the fact that about 25% of the police officers who are killed each year are murdered with their own guns (Brown and Langan, 2001). From the first day of the police academy, officers are reminded that every time they are in a hand-to-hand physical confrontation with a suspect, the confrontation involves a gun (the officer's weapon).

Force Options — *Less than Lethal (batons)*

Most police agencies issue their officers some type of baton as a use-of-force option. These are typically described as impact weapons because they are intended to gain compliance by causing pain or injury, but it is also accurate to state they are intended to have an impact on people's behavior simply by their display or presence. They include the traditional wooden nightstick or the aluminum PR-24, and the ASP, which is a flexible metal rod that telescopes out to full length.

The PR-24, like the ASP, is available as an expandable baton. With the flick of the wrist, the officer can expand the baton to its full length. The major advantage of the expandable baton is that it is carried easily on the duty belt and thus always available, unlike the non-collapsible models which are easily left in patrol cars or lockers (Nowicki, 2001b).

Although generally described as "less than lethal," batons can constitute a form of deadly force. Training protocols for batons identify areas of the body where baton strikes should be directed, depending on the situation (Monadnock..., 1998). A strike to the head or other vulnerable area would be justified only in a deadly-force situation (see Figure 1).

In the 1970s, the city of Detroit took nightsticks away from its police. This left Detroit officers with no official impact weapon, and some began using metal flashlights for that purpose. In 1993, after the well-publicized case of Malice Green, who was killed by police officers who struck him the head with metal flashlights, Detroit officers were prohibited from carrying metal flashlights. A Detroit citizen panel formed in the aftermath of a police shooting case in 2001 is now recommending that all Detroit officers be issued ASP batons (Hanson, 2001).

Impact weapons have a psychological effect as well. The mere display of a baton may bring compliance. Whether this type of display should be reported as a use of force is subject to debate. However, a Department of Justice document recently recommended that officers be required to report all "shows of force" (U.S. DOJ, 2001b).

Force Options — *Less than Lethal (other impact options)*

In chapter 2, when Officer Joe Beatcop responded to the mental patient cutting himself on the town square, the situation was resolved with a beanbag shotgun. From a safe distance, Joe was able to immobilize the man, thus allowing other officers to safely control him.

Less-than-lethal rounds vary from small liquid projectiles to sponge balls to beanbags, (small cloth bags filled with metal pellets). A newer option is the Pepperball round, a small projectile fired from a distance. The pepperball disintegrates on impact, releasing pepper spray. All these types of projectiles can be fired with a variety of weapons including conventional shotguns ("Less Lethal," 2001).

The primary advantage of this type of force option is that police can use these weapons from a safe distance. Disabling a violent person from 30 or 40 feet away is safer for both officers and the suspect than an up-close and physical confrontation, which could have serious or even fatal consequences.

However, describing these options as less-than-lethal somewhat understates the risks involved. While officers are trained to avoid the head area when using these weapons, most often the people being shot at are not static targets. They may be running or moving erratically. A round aimed at the chest may end up striking the person in the face, a potentially fatal shot.

Using less-than-lethal force options is not risk-free for police officers either. Consider an officer using a beanbag shotgun to disable a man with a knife. If the round either misses or has no effect, the man may charge the officer. The officer's ability to get his gun out his holster, a reasonable use of force in this situation, would be impaired because his hands are tied up with the shotgun.

Force Options — *Less than Lethal (electronic weapons)*

Popularly known as "stun guns," these electronic weapons have been in use in police departments around the country for years. They work in one of two ways. The first type shoots out metal barbs or probes that stick in the clothes or skin of the person targeted. The probes are attached to the weapon by thin wires, and by pushing a button the officer sends a charge of electricity through the person, temporarily immobilizing him.

The second type is sold widely as a personal protection device. The electric charge is applied by touching the stun gun directly onto the body of the offending party.

Figure 1. Monadnock Baton Chart[1]

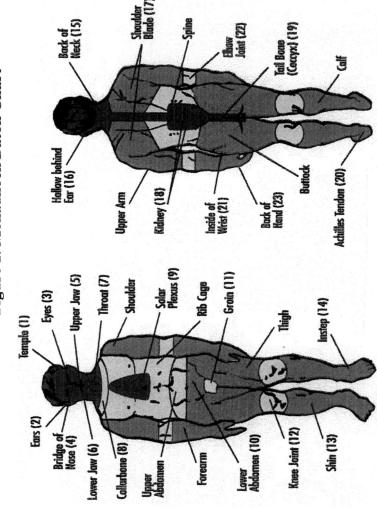

Reprinted with permission of Monadnock Lifetime Products, Inc., Fitzwilliam, NH.

The benefits of these devices include their acceptance by courts as a safe and non-injurious option. They require minimal training and are highly effective. An application of electricity through the device will usually cause total immobilization in two to five seconds (Jones, 2001).

The downside is that these devices must be deployed within a certain distance, generally between 15 to 21 feet. The barbs flare out when fired, and if used at distances beyond 21 feet, one or both barbs are likely to miss the person. Within 15 feet, an officer is at increased risk for a sudden charge by the person.

As with the remote beanbag-type rounds, the major problem is that the subjects of these weapons generally refuse to stand still and provide a good target.

Force Options — *Firearms*

A police officer's firearm is the ultimate deadly-force option. In addition to the handgun, officers are likely to have access to shotguns and/or rifles, either stored in the trunk or secured in a rack inside the passenger compartment.

A department's policy on firearms may dictate the specific handgun officers may carry, may allow them to carry more than handgun at a time, may allow different weapons based on assignment, or may give officers a choice of handguns to select from.

The department's decisions and policy on firearms may have a serious impact on police use of force. For example, in 1988 the Washington DC police issued its officers Glock nine millimeter semi-auto pistols. Among firearms experts, the Glock was known to have a sensitive trigger. A *Washington Post* investigation found the number of accidental discharges by Washington, DC police officers in 1994 exceeded both New York's and Chicago's, both much larger police departments. The Post alleged lax training by the D.C. police. "A Washington Post investigation found that 75 percent of all D.C. officers involved in shootings during 1996 failed to comply with the retraining regulation. One officer waited so long to come to the range that firearms instructors found a spider nest growing inside his Glock" (Leen and Horwitz, 1998, p.A-1).

Summary

The decisions on exactly what force options to provide to officers are vital. These decisions have not only economic implications, but carry training and supervisory consequences as well. Decision makers, whether political leaders or police managers, should make these choices carefully and with complete recognition of their importance.

Thousands of times each day, police officers across the country will be involved in a variety of incidents where they will choose from the force options provided. The safety of officers and citizens, and to some extent the fabric of the community, are dependent on the outcome of these encounters.

Even more important than the selection of tools provided is the wisdom to make the right choices. The art of policing combines legal knowledge, ethics, and physical skills with the courage to apply the appropriate force, and no more, at the proper moment.

Discussion Questions

(1) Do you agree that physical presence is important in police officers? If so, should size be a factor in choosing police officers?

(2) In your opinion, should there be fitness standards for police officers?

(3) Why not provide police officers with as many force options as possible? Other than cost, what factors might go into these equipment decisions?

(4) Would you support a force policy that required police officers to use less lethal methods prior to using deadly force? Why or why not?

Notes

1. Areas in solid black sustain a minimal level of resultant trauma. Except for the head, neck and spine, the whole body is in this category for the application of baton blocking and restraint skills. Areas of white sustain a moderate to serious level of resultant trauma, which tends to be more long lasting, but may also be temporary. Areas in grey — including the head, neck, spine and tail bone — sustain the highest level of resultant trauma. Injuries in this last area tend to range from serious to long lasting, and may include unconsciousness, serious bodily injury, shock or death.

Chapter 6. Making the Right Choices

"A lot of people these days wanted to think of police work as being mostly polite, of force being used according to the rules of etiquette. They wanted to be protected unobtrusively, and totally without violence."

Robert Daley (1988)

How do police know what type and level of force to use in each situation? Police recruits learn early on that in a force situation they may use the degree of force that is "reasonable." That sounds simple enough, but applying that standard in practice is difficult.

Take, for instance, the common police radio run to the scene of a "man with a knife." What level of force would a reasonable officer be prepared to use in this situation? Clearly, much more information is needed, including: What exactly is the person's behavior? Is the knife in his hand or concealed on his person? Is the person actively threatening others? Has he or she cut someone? What kind of knife is it? What other people are around? Is the person outside in public or inside a residence? There are a number of factors that will go into whatever decision a reasonable officer makes.

In an effort to provide guidance to police officers in these situations, researchers and police agencies developed what are commonly referred to as Use-of-Force Continuums. These continuums may be as simple as a listing of force alternatives, as in Figure 2.

More sophisticated continuums attempt to calibrate the force used by the officer to the actions of the suspect. Figure 3 is a simple version of this type of force continuum.

While these types of continuums were designed to provide guidance to the police officer, even a cursory review shows them to be lacking. The first question that occurs is: What if the force option suggested doesn't work? Let's suppose that the officer's command is met with a verbal suggestion to the cop to commit a sexual act on himself. Does that indicate that the officer is entitled to move up the continuum? If not, does that mean the use of repeated, perhaps stronger verbal commands? If so, does the suspect's continued verbal defiance now constitute passive resistance?

Figure 2. Police Use-of-Force Continuum

No force

Officers' presence in uniform

Verbal communication

Light subject control, escort techniques, pressure point control, handcuffs

Chemical agents

Physical tactics and use of weapons other than chemicals and firearms

Firearms/deadly force

If verbal commands fail, should the officer now put hands on the suspect, an "escort hold" for example? What if the suspect is 6'5" and the officer is 5'5"? Is that really the best choice? Would a reasonable officer ignore the peril of a physical confrontation with a much larger suspect?

Figure 3. Use-of-Force Continuum Resistance and Response Levels

Suspect Resistance Level	Officer Level of Control (Force)
Suspect presence	Interview stance
Verbal resistance	Verbal commands
Passive resistance	Transport techniques
Defensive resistance	Chemical agents
Active physical resistance	Physical tactics/weapons
Firearms/deadly force	Firearms/deadly force

Source: Alpert and Smith (1999).

It's clear that these situations are much more complex than can be captured in the continuums above.

FLETC Model

Two other continuum models more successfully address the complexity issue. The first is the use-of-force model developed by the Federal Law Enforcement Training Center (FLETC). FLETC is the unit responsible for much of the training of federal law enforcement officers, including Drug Enforcement Administration, Immigration and Naturalization Services, and Secret Service officers, among others. The FLETC model (Figure 4) is significantly more complex than those presented above.

Research verifies the common sense notion that "the single best predictor of police use of force is whether the suspect used force" (McEwen, 1996:41). The FLETC model attempts to capture that dynamic by listing suspect behavior as either compliant, actively resistant or passively resistant, assaultive (trying to cause physical harm), or highly assaultive (attempting to cause serious physical harm or death).

Figure 4. Federal Law Enforcement Training Center Use-of-Force Model

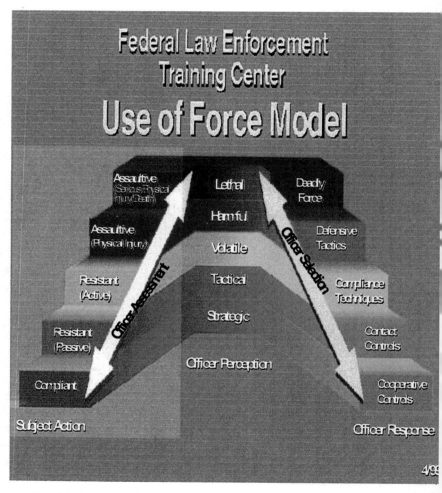

(Reprinted with permission of the FLETC.)

Figure 5. The Action-Response Use-of-Force Continuum

IMPORTANT - The list of officer responses is **not** intended to be in any specific order, but reflects on the amount of resistance encountered. The officer will choose the necessary response to gain control of the situation based on departmental policy, his/her physical capabilities, perception, training, and experience.

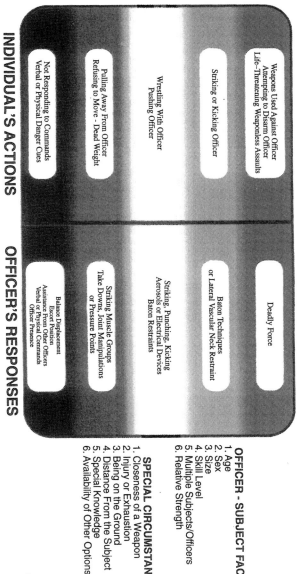

INDIVIDUAL'S ACTIONS

- Not Responding to Commands
- Verbal or Physical Danger Cues

- Pulling Away From Officer
- Refusing to Move - Dead Weight

- Wrestling With Officer
- Pushing Officer

- Striking or Kicking Officer

- Weapons Used Against Officer
- Attempting to Disarm Officer
- Life–Threatening Weaponless Assaults

OFFICER'S RESPONSES

- Balance Displacement
- Escort Position
- Assistance From Other Officers
- Verbal or Physical Commands
- Officer Presence

- Striking Muscle Groups
- Take Downs, Joint Manipulations
- or Pressure Points

- Striking, Punching, Kicking
- Aerosols or Electrical Devices
- Baton Restraints

- Baton Techniques
- or Lateral Vascular Neck Restraint

- Deadly Force

OFFICER - SUBJECT FACTORS

1. Age
2. Sex
3. Size
4. Skill Level
5. Multiple Subjects/Officers
6. Relative Strength

SPECIAL CIRCUMSTANCES

1. Closeness of a Weapon
2. Injury or Exhaustion
3. Being on the Ground
4. Distance From the Subject
5. Special Knowledge
6. Availability of Other Options

Continuum of Arrest: Control – Handcuff – Search – Evaluate – Transport

(Reprinted with the permission of Samuel Faulkner.)

On the opposite side is officer reaction, ranging from cooperative controls, contact controls, compliance techniques, defensive tactics and deadly force. At the lower end of the continuum, cooperative and contact controls include officer presence and verbalizations, which are used in the majority of police interactions with cooperative or passively resisting people. Where suspects are passively resisting, stronger verbal commands or simple hands-on techniques might be appropriate.

As opposed to the model shown in Figure 2 — which attempts to match specific options to "offender behavior" — the FLETC model uses general terms that might include several specific options or tools for the officer. Compliance techniques include strong verbal commands, grabbing the individual and physically guiding or moving him, pressure points, or other physical moves or holds intended to cause pain and gain compliance. The FLETC model distinguishes between "resistant" and "assaultive" behavior. When a person moves from simply resisting officer action and begins attempting to cause injury to the officer, the officer moves to defensive tactics, not only blocking the person's attacks but responding with strikes and blows of his own. This could include punches or knee strikes by the officer or use of a baton or nightstick. Chemical irritant would also be an option. The particular option is based on the officer's assessment of how serious the attack is. If the suspect's assaultive behavior becomes more serious — such as use of a weapon against the officer — or the officer is in danger of serious physical injury, deadly force becomes an option.

The model emphasizes assessment of the individual's action and the officer's response to that action. The bridge between the two is the officer's perception.

Action-Response Continuum

Another model of interest is the Action-Response Use-of-Force Continuum developed by Samuel Faulkner. Faulkner is the defensive tactics trainer for the Ohio Peace Officer Training Commission (OPOTC) in London, OH. OPOTC is the certifying body for police training in Ohio, and Faulkner frequently testifies as an expert witness in excessive force cases.

Faulkner developed his continuum by trying to answer the question of what would a reasonable officer do in various force situations.

Faulkner developed various use-of-force scenarios, and then asked officers to react to them by listing what they thought would be reasonable force responses. Faulkner developed his scenarios using various elements to duplicate factors identified in the Graham v. Conner (1989) decision. Thus, Faulkner believes his continuum represents the best effort to describe what reasonable officers would do in various situations "if all other things are equal." However, as Faulkner eloquently notes, "The truth is that all things are never equal" (Faulkner, 1999:6).

As part of his model, Faulkner also lists two other categories of factors that might influence the officer's use-of-force decision making. The first is "Officer-Subject Factors," which include age, sex, size, skill level, multiple subjects/officers, and relative strength.

The second category Faulkner describes as "Special Circumstances," which include closeness of weapon, injury or exhaustion, and being on the ground.

The Action-Response Continuum is read from the bottom to the top. As the civilian's actions escalate, the officer reacts by selecting from among the force options listed. Figure 5 shows the Action-Response model.

Like the FLETC model, the Action-Response model allows the officer to calibrate his use of force based not only on suspect behavior but other factors as well.

Force Options Decision Making

It is apparent that both of the preceding models were developed with a recognition of the complexity of force decision making. Both attempt to capture the multitude of factors present in these situations, and both try to organize these factors in a coherent fashion providing guidance to the police officer that is as specific as possible.

In essence, what the creators of these two models attempted to do was to define, as precisely as possible, what a reasonable officer would do in various situations. Yet in Graham v. Connor (1989), the Supreme Court noted that "the test of reasonableness under the Fourth Amendment is not capable of precise definition or mechanical application."

Ultimately, this is where any continuum model falls short. It is simply not possible to devise a model that will account for the host of factors involved in making use-of-force decisions. Use-of-force decision making is simply too complex to fit into the limited framework of a continuum model.

For example, consider the multitude of factors that go into as simple a phrase as "officer presence." Are we talking about a single officer or multiple officers? Are we talking about a physically imposing officer who looks similar to an NFL linebacker? Are we talking about an officer who exudes competence or one who is more suited to a Richard Simmons workout tape?

In fact, in force situations, 10 reasonable officers may make 10 different force choices. Reasonableness is not a specific point on a continuum, but a range of options. What may be an option for the 15-year police veteran with a strong tactical background may not be a reasonable option for the rookie officer just out of the academy. Moreover, Officer A, confronted with very similar situations at different points in his career, may make very different choices.

Training and physical conditioning are also factors. The officer with a high level of skill in using a baton is more likely to choose that as an option. An officer in poor physical condition, knowing he will likely not be successful in an extended physical encounter, may well resort to higher levels of force more quickly.

In addition, not all force tools are equally available at all times. A shotgun locked in a patrol car is not an option for an officer attempting to control a violent suspect inside a residence. Even in a deadly-force situation, a firearm may not be an appropriate choice in a room full of people.

There are, however, some general guidelines which govern officer action and become the foundation on which to judge individual incidents.

- Officers may use only that level of force that is reasonably necessary, and no more. What was reasonable will be based on that individual situation and all the various factors involved. While it is difficult to define, "reasonable" covers a lot of territory. Unreasonable or excessive force is something like pornography. We usually know it when we see it.

- The reasonableness of the force used will reflect not only the amount of resistance encountered, but also factors related to the officer and civilian involved as well. In the wording of the Supreme Court, the incident will be judged on the "totality of circumstances." Good officers, with training and experience, will be able to clearly articulate these factors.

- Officer action is NOT dictated solely by suspect behavior. Suspect behavior obviously is a major factor limiting officer alternatives, but officers almost always have some decision making to do. Even the worst case gunfights will involve decisions on cover, concealment, and choice of weapon.

Decision Making under Stress

Choosing the appropriate level of force is clearly a complex decision. Yet the more difficult issue is the fact that these decisions must be made under stress, and on occasion, extraordinary stress.

There is wide recognition that stress affects physical performance. The easiest analogy is athletic competition. Particularly at the professional level, the contests come down not to physical skills, but to which athlete or team can best perform under pressure. Performance under pressure is what makes great athlete, the

Michael Jordan or John Elway. The best performers thrive under pressure while the rest wilt.

The 2001 U.S. Open Golf Championship is a perfect example. On the final day of the tournament, two golfers were on the eighteenth green putting for the championship. Stewart Cink missed a three-foot putt, thus opening the door for Retief Goosen of South Africa. Goosen was putting from 12 feet away and with a two-putt would win the championship. His first putt went by the hole, leaving him a two footer for the championship. To the amazement of every hacker who ever broke 100, Goosen then missed the two footer, forcing a playoff the next day.

What happened? There is no doubt about the physical ability of these golfers to make those putts. They *were* feeling some intense pressure. A major tournament, millions of people watching on television, and a huge money purse at stake all contributed to the stress these two must have experienced. Under pressure, they couldn't perform. In sports parlance, they "choked."

Now imagine a police officer in a serious use-of-force situation. While there may ultimately be money involved in a civil suit years down the road, the stakes are much more immediate and much more personal. The officer may be facing serious injury or death, and is face-to-face with the choice to harm or kill another human being. He or she will make a decision in a matter of seconds that will reverberate through the community and affect that officer for the rest of his or her life. That officer must not only make the right decision, but physically perform, implementing that decision correctly using the tool or tools chosen.

Research has long linked physical or mental stress with changes in physical performance (Tutko and Tose, 1976). Physical performance can be divided into three categories, the first being fine motor skills. Fine motor skills involve hand/eye coordination and hand dexterity. Examples would be playing a piano or shooting accurately with a handgun.

The second category of physical performance is gross motor skills, defined as simple strength skills, punching or jumping. This is the category where performance may actually be improved under stress. Some football players, as an example, may "psych" themselves up prior to the game, try to get the adrenaline flowing, working up anger and fear in an attempt to maximize their strength and speed. Yet for the athlete needing to do more than a simple test of strength — such as shooting a foul shot, fielding a ground ball, or putting for a championship — this type of self-induced stress would be counterproductive.

The third category of physical performance is complex motor skills, involving different muscle groups in complex movements involving tracking or timing. Throwing a forward pass in football, or driving a golf ball would be examples. Complex motor skills involve cognitive or thinking activity and decision making. They are not instinctual.

Stress effects are predictable based on escalating heart rates. "Scientists found that high or even moderate levels of stress interfere with fine muscular control and decision-making. In contrast, motor skills dominated by large muscle groups, that have minimal fine motor control and very little decision-making or cognitive complexity, are not affected by high levels of stress. Studies have also found that fine motor skills deteriorate at 115 Beats per Minute (BPM), complex motor skills deteriorate at 145 BPM" (Siddle, 1999:3).

Even at a relatively low level of stress, 115 BPM, an officer's ability to shoot accurately is compromised. This is an important point to understand in the face of unrealistic expectations that police should shoot to wound, targeting arms or legs. The fine motor skills that would allow precision shooting are the first physical casualties of stress.

Perhaps more importantly, as stress increases decision making or critical thinking skills begin to deteriorate.

Under extreme stress, the physiological effects are marked. "When the brain perceives an imminent deadly-force threat, the sympathetic nervous system (SNS) is activated involuntarily, resulting in an immediate discharge of stress hormones" (Siddle, p.1).

This activation of the SNS is what has commonly been termed the "fight or flight" reaction. The SNS-related chemical soup of stress hormones released into the body have significant physiological impacts. For example, vision is profoundly affected. Depth perception and night vision are disrupted.

Under major stress, a person's field of vision (peripheral vision) may be narrowed as much as 70% (Siddle, p.2). This is the phenomenon commonly referred to as "tunnel vision." As Siddle point outs "...consider that vision is the mother of all senses and is the primary sensory source on which the brain relies in combat"[1] (Siddle, p.1).

Threat Response

There are three basic steps required for officers facing serious threats. First is threat recognition. Based on visual and other cues, the officer must accurately and quickly comprehend the nature and seriousness of the threat. Second is decision making on the nature of his/her response, choosing the proper tool or tools. And finally, the officer must physically perform to implement the force response chosen.

Consider some of the specific consequences of the stress-related vision changes. The loss of depth-perception could lead an officer to believing a threat is much closer physically than it is in reality. "Tunnel vision" might lead to an officer failing to see either innocent bystanders on the periphery of the incident or potential threats from other civilians located outside his narrowed vision. Poor night vision could lead to officers misidentifying subtle or quick movements.

Lack of clarity in recognizing and interpreting threats could have fatal consequences for police officers and those they confront. Misinterpreting behavior by a suspect could lead the officer to use deadly force when, in reality, it was not warranted. Conversely, an officer's failure to accurately identify a real deadly threat could have fatal consequences for that officer as well.

Developing police officers with the ability to accurately identify the threats they face, make good decisions in the face of those threats, and then skillfully implement their decisions under extreme stress is the challenge facing police trainers across the country.

Discussion Questions

(1) The Department of Justice is recommending that all police departments develop a use-of-force continuum. What do you see as the pros and cons of such a tool?

(2) Should extreme stress provide a legal defense for police officers who mistakenly kill someone in a use-of-force situation?

(3) Describe a force incident you are familiar with. Consider the three steps of threat recognition, decision making in response, and physical implementation of the decision and apply them to this situation.

Notes

1. Siddle (1999) deliberately uses the term "combat" to refer to serious police force incidents. The stress dynamics and physiological consequences are the same.

Chapter 7. Use-of-Force Training

"In their handling of criminals and armed gangsters, ignorance and a lack of training and understanding are defined as being the causes of the frequency of police discomfiture."

Charles Reith, *The Blind Eye of History* (1952)

Over the course of a day, a police officer may act as a marriage counselor, children's protective worker, legal advisor, clergy member, traffic engineer and psychologist. All these roles are an important part of police work, and training should prepare officers to competently handle the wide variety of problems police confront. Yet the one thing that separates police officers from all other professions is the authority and the responsibility to use force. The fact that force is the central element of the police role colors all interactions an officer has with people in the community.

Use-of-force issues are woven throughout police training. Whether the topic is legal issues, ethics, cultural diversity or firearms, appropriate use of force is a dominant theme. Use-of-force training must include a grounding in constitutional and legal concepts, a deep grounding in human behavior, broad appreciation of cultural differences, and excellent communications skills, particularly involving mediation techniques.

Complementing this knowledge base is training on the physical skills involved in police work — firearms use, defensive tactics, safe driving, and first aid. Long gone are the days when new officers were handed a nightstick, badge, and a gun, and after a few days with a senior officer they were deemed ready for street patrol.

In 1952, according to a survey of 33 police departments around the country, the average time spent in recruit training was

Figure 6: Ohio Peace Officer Training Commission Basic Training Curriculum

TOPIC — ADMINISTRATION.......................................21 Hours

Introduction, Role of American Peace Officer, Philosophy & Principles of the American Justice System, The Criminal Justice System and Structure of the American Courts, Community Policing, Ethics & Professionalism, Introduction to Report Writing.

TOPIC — LEGAL ....77 Hours

General Provisions, Ohio Revised Code (Criminal), Laws of Arrest, Search & Seizure, Legal Aspects of Interview & Interrogation, Civil Liability and Use of Force, Testifying in Court & Rules of Evidence.

TOPIC — HUMAN RELATIONS ....76 Hours

Communicating with the Public & the Media, Handling the Special Needs Population, Domestic Violence, Crisis Intervention, Child Abuse & Neglect, Missing Children Investigation, Juvenile Justice System, Victims Rights, Crime Prevention, Understanding Cultural Differences.

TOPIC — FIREARMS ....60 Hours

Safety Procedures, Handgun and Related Equipment, Basic Fundamentals of Pistol Craft, One Hand Technique, Multiple Targets, Low Level Light Conditions, Use of Protective Cover, Move and Shoot, Shotgun Training.

TOPIC — DRIVING ....24 Hours

Defensive Driving, Pursuit Driving, Practical Exercises.

TOPIC — SUBJECT CONTROL....................................34 Hours

Subject Control Techniques, Intermediate Weapons.

TOPIC — FIRST AID ....16 Hours

TOPIC — PATROL..49 Hours

Vehicle Patrol Techniques, foot Patrol, Responding to Crimes in Progress, Building Searches, Stops and Approaches, Auto Theft & VIN Reconstruction, Gang Awareness, Communications, Prisoner Booking and Handling, Report Writing.

TOPIC — CIVIL DISORDERS.......................................17 Hours

Control of Nonviolent Crowds, Confronting Hostile Crowds, Riot Formations, Chemical Agents, Bombs & Explosives, Terrorism — Domestic and International, Hazardous Materials.

TOPIC — TRAFFIC...91 Hours

Motor Vehicle Offenses, Commercial Vehicle Offenses, Traffic Crash Investigation, Traffic Enforcement Technologies, Traffic Direction & Control, Alcohol Detection, apprehension and Prosecution, Exercise for Traffic Crash Investigation.

TOPIC — INVESTIGATIONS ....55 Hours

Crime Scene Search, Evidence Collection Techniques, Crime Scene Sketching, Police Photography, Tracing Stolen Property, Arson Scene Investigation, Controlled Substance & Drug Awareness, Ohio Drug Laws, Confidential Informants, Observation, Perception, and Description, Line-Ups, Gambling & Prostitution, Liquor Control & Enforcement, Surveillance, Interview & Interrogation Techniques, Search Warrants, Investigative Report Writing.

TOPIC — PHYSICAL CONDITIONING.......................30 Hours

342 hours. By 1982, the average time spent in recruit training, including field training, had grown to 633 hours (Thibault et al., 2001). In 1993, a U.S. Bureau of Justice Statistics survey of 12,000 municipal and county law enforcement agencies found, on average, a requirement of 425 academy hours and 215 field training hours (ibid., p.353).

In 2002, the typical police academy curriculum generally required between 500 and 700 hours. For example, the basic academy training program for police officers in Ohio is 550 hours. Figure 6 provides a breakdown of the mandatory topics covered in the 550 hours (Ohio Peace..., 2000). In California, the minimum police officer academy training program is 599 hours. Figure 7 provides a breakdown of those hours (California Commission..., 2001).

Recruit academy training is typically followed by a field training program lasting anywhere from eight to 22 weeks.

Setting the Context

A listing of topics in a police academy curriculum does not adequately describe the complexity of recruit training. A great deal of the training experience is acculturation, that is trying on the role of police officer to ensure a proper fit.

Like the orientation of a new employee in any organization, the first order of business in recruit training is an introduction to the culture of the agency. The mission and values of police organizations around the country may vary, but the themes are similar.

The mission statement of the Illinois State Patrol reads: "The Illinois State Patrol will promote public safety with integrity, service and pride to improve the quality of life for our citizens."

The mission statement of the Miami Township Police Department, a small agency in southwest Ohio, states: "Miami Township Police Department shall faithfully serve all people within our jurisdiction with dignity, equality and compassion."

Figure 7: Content and Minimum Hourly Requirements — California, 2000

Topic	Hours	Topic	Hours
History, Professionalism and Ethics	8	Vehicle Pullovers	14
Criminal Justice System	4	Crimes in Progress	16
Community Relations	12	Handling Disputes/Crowd Control	12
Victimology/Crisis Interventions	6	Domestic Violence	8
Introduction to Criminal Law	6	Unusual Occurrences	4
Crimes Against Property	10	Missing Persons	4
Crimes Against Persons	10	Traffic Enforcement	22
General Criminal Statutes	4	Traffic Accident Investigation	12
Crimes Against Children	6	Preliminary Investigation	4
Sex Crimes	6	Custody	4
Juvenile Law and Procedure	6	Physical Fitness/Officer Stress	40
Controlled Substances	12	Person Searches, Baton, etc.	60
ABC Law	4	First Aid and CPR	21
Laws of Arrest	12	Information Systems	4
Search and Seizure	12	Persons with Disabilities	6
Presentation of Evidence	8	Gang Awareness	8
Investigative Report Writing	40	Crimes Against the Justice System	4
Vehicle Operations	24	Weapons Violations	4
Use of Force	12	Hazardous Materials	4
Patrol Techniques	12	Cultural Diversity	24
		Minimum Instruction Hours Total 599	

Hartford, Connecticut's mission statement says: "The Hartford Police Department serves to enhance the quality of life in the City of Hartford by developing partnerships with the community, and the other stakeholders in a manner that promotes problem solving and preserves a safe environment through professional law enforcement that respects human dignity."

The North Cambria Regional Police of Pennsylvania has a somewhat distinctive mission statement in that it directly refers to police use of force: "The mission of the North Cambria Regional Police is to provide quality public service based on high ethical and professional standards. The mission is to be attained through a sincere commitment to public service. It includes preserving the peace and order of the Municipality through conflict management and enforcement of criminal laws and quasi-criminal laws by officers who are committed to the rule of law and have a unique authority to investigate, arrest, search, seize, and use reasonable and necessary force. It includes being both responsive and responsible to the public we serve. Our mission is public service and we are proud of it."

Much of the military regimen that characterizes police training is an attempt to inculcate these values. The Missouri State Highway Patrol Academy is typical. On their first day at the police academy, recruits are told that lesson number one is, "The first and last word out of your mouth is 'Sir' or 'Ma'am'" (Biram, 2002). This conditioning in basic courtesy is particularly challenging for the large percentage of recruits who have never uttered "Sir" or "Ma'am" in their lives.

The process also addresses physical appearance. The officers-in-training dress in uniforms that identify them as police recruits. Appearing in public, in a police uniform, can be jarring. Adaptation to constant public scrutiny must be experienced in training and understood as a crucial element of the police experience.

The academy emphasis on self-discipline, teamwork, courtesy, respect and professionalism constitute the context for use-of-force training. Without strong self-discipline, operating in the stressful environment of policing, officers could allow their emotions to govern their behavior and overwhelm their commitment to professionalism and respect.

Courtesy is a key value with a direct relationship to use of force. The basic principle is not complicated. An FBI publication notes: "Officers who treat citizens with respect receive respect in return. Therefore, when officers stop or arrest citizens, it is critical that they do not treat these individuals in a manner that adds to their anger, fear, or embarrassment. Simple courtesy on the part of officers softens these emotions" (Wadman and Ziman, 1993).

The values of professionalism, respect, courtesy, dignity, and service all provide the framework within which use-of-force training is accomplished. It is only in the context of these values that the recruit can fully understand the magnitude of the authority and responsibility to use force against fellow citizens. New York writer Heather MacDonald eloquently captured the challenge after a study of the New York City Police Department Academy: "Education at the Academy is a model of how to integrate rigorous tactical instruction with an unequivocal mandate of communication and service" (MacDonald, 2000:46).

Developing the Physical Skills

All force options are skill-based and can be improved with repetition and practice. This is obviously the case with firearms or baton training. Yet practice and training are no less important in developing command presence, that sense of competence and control that characterizes good police officers. Command presence is accomplished by posture and bearing, voice control and tone, and effective non-verbal behaviors. Officers who appear timid, uncertain or unsure of themselves are more likely to face challenges than officers who exude professional competence.

The failure to develop that professional demeanor can be fatal. In an FBI study of offenders who killed police officers, one significant factor discovered was the offenders' feeling that the victimized officers, as one offender put it, "looked easy" (Pinizzotto and Davis, 1999).

In one case, the offender, having made the decision to murder a cop, began roaming the streets looking for an officer to kill. He shortly came across a uniformed sergeant who was in a service station having a tire repair done on his patrol car. However, the offender decided the sergeant "looked too difficult to take." Asked to clarify what he meant by this statement, "the offender stated that he (the police officer) was not particularly large in size or menacing in appearance but 'just looked like he could handle himself'" (ibid.).

A short time later, the offender found another police officer, "casually walked over to the officer and struck him with his fist. As the officer fell to the ground, the offender removed the officer's service weapon and shot him six times" (ibid.).

Interpersonal communication is one of the most complex and difficult challenges all of us face. Even with those we care deeply about, under the best conditions, face-to-face communications are often a problem. Cops are charged with trying to effectively communicate with people who are sometimes hostile, often under the influence of alcohol and drugs, under extreme stress, and occasionally physically combative.

While some people seem blessed with the ability to effectively communicate with other people, this is a rare quality. Yet effective communication is a set of skills that can be learned. Police officers are trained in a variety of communications skills, including crisis intervention, negotiations, and mediation techniques. Many of the same skills displayed by good teachers, good therapists, and good business leaders are applicable to police work. There are a number of training approaches under a variety of names like "Tactical Communications," "Conflict Management Training" and others that attempt to improve officer skills in this area.

Experience will add to and refine the skills taught in the academy. Good cops develop a variety of techniques to defuse situations, and they also learn that communications techniques that work in family therapy in a social worker's office might not be so effective with an enraged husband in his own living room.

As one example, most counselors recognize the importance of letting people express their emotions. Allowing a person the opportunity for catharsis or venting of his or her emotions is generally believed to be a constructive step in communicating with a distraught or emotionally upset person. Yet this same principle may not translate to situations confronted by police officers. "Contrary to conventional wisdom, letting someone 'vent' may be the worst thing you can do... Studies have found that letting people vent during these situations can actually increase the probability of incident escalation" (McCaffery, 2001:26).

There are at least two interpersonal communications skills programs designed specifically for police officers. Management of Aggressive Behavior (MOAB) was developed by Roland Ouellette, a former Connecticut state trooper. The program emphasizes recognition of non-verbal behavior and management of aggressive behavior. Ouellette says, "Understanding body language and recognizing the signals can prepare you for an attack before it occurs, end the confrontation before it begins, and help you win the encounter without physical confrontation" (Nowicki, 2001a:27).

Another popular program is Verbal Judo, an approach developed by George Thompson, a martial arts expert and former police officer. Thompson redefines judo techniques as verbal tactics and teaches them as tools to de-escalate potentially violent situations in the street (Thompson, 1983).

As with good officer presence, the basic principle in both these programs is that effective communication skills in volatile situations will reduce the necessity to use more forceful measures.

Proficiency in the physical skills involved in handling batons and using chemical irritant, firearms, and other force options is crucial. Like any physical skill, the only way to achieve a high level of effectiveness is learning proper technique combined with practice. Proficiency with each weapon is only part of the picture. The Supreme Court's language describing force situations as "fast evolving, tense, and uncertain" (Graham v. Connor, 1989) succinctly captures the problem. Officers must be prepared to instantly transition from one option to another.

For example, a man is sprayed with chemical irritant and after a second's hesitation, charges the officer. The situation calls for the officer to transition quickly to another force option, baton or Taser as an example. This transition consists of a number of discrete physical acts that must be accomplished quickly and efficiently. As with all these skills, the path to success is practice.

Officers also must carry out multiple physical tasks simultaneously. They may be giving verbal commands, spraying chemical irritant, and calling for backup all at the same time. As with the individual skills involved, performing multiple tasks effectively requires practice.

Decision Making under Stress

The essence of police work is doing. Sitting in a classroom listening to a lecture is not adequate preparation for effective policing, particularly for high-level performance in use-of-force situations.

Police training in general is increasingly moving to an adult-centered learning model emphasizing problem solving and role playing scenarios as the primary style of learning. A pioneer in this training approach is the Royal Canadian Mounted Police (RCMP). This "learn by doing" approach has wide application in police training, but nowhere more clearly than in the use of force. An RCMP trainer observing recruits trained in the new model notes: "Risk assessment and coming up with levels of force options became second nature" (Weinblatt, 1999:89).

Effective handling of stress is the key factor in use-of-force training. As has been described previously, even moderate levels of stress can have deleterious impact on physical performance and decision-making ability. Training recruits to perform under stress is the major challenge in police academies.

Realism is certainly an important factor in use-of-force training. A certain degree of artificiality cannot be overcome, as even the best designed training will be handicapped by the recruit's knowledge that it is in fact training. Yet several steps can be taken to enhance realism.

Early stages of training dwell on understanding the professional context of use of force as well as mastery of the physical skills involved in force options. Once the context is understood and the physical skills mastered, trainers can begin using simple scenarios. After each scenario the recruit is debriefed with an emphasis on recognition and articulation of the legal and tactical issues involved in the situation.

As recruits progress through the training, the scenarios may be become more complex, with recruits making use-of-force choices. Again, the debriefing must reinforce good decision making. Trainers can begin to add stress to the exercises. This can be accomplished by adding noise (loud music, sirens, or car horns) and increasing the physical stress by forcing the recruits to perform physical exercise prior to the scenario. The increase in heart rate will mimic some of the same physiological effects of stress. Physical fitness is a key element of the training, as improving fitness levels will mitigate some of the physiological stress effects.

The training should be moved out of the sterile academy atmosphere into more realistic settings. Where possible, the settings should reflect the multitude of unfriendly environments where officers will work.

Mark Gajdostik, an Oregon police officer and defensive tactics instructor suggests that trainers move the scenarios to locations that approximate the work conditions police officers face. "Drug houses, trash filled alleys, dark and narrow hallways, urine soaked stairways, busy highways...the list could go on and on. How often is training done or simulated on a slippery surface, in darkened hallways, in blinding sunlight, with sirens blaring?" (Gajdostik, 2001).

Competent performance in this type of scenario should be mandatory for completion of the academy. With the experience gained through training, most recruits' performance will notably improve. There will be recruits who will be unable to perform under stress and this will become apparent as the academy training progresses. For these individuals, the choice of a different vocation is in everyone's best interest.

Psychological Preparation for Use of Force

Much of the literature on use of force is concentrated on control of excessive force by police. Improved training, citizen review panels, early warning systems, community-based policing and a variety of criminal and civil legal actions are all suggested as possible remedies to rein in brutal cops. This emphasis on control of excessive force obscures what in fact may be a larger use-of-force problem seldom discussed outside of police circles — the *reluctance* by police officers to use force, especially deadly force, when necessary.

For example, on January 12, 1998, at about 5:30pm, a Lauens County, Georgia deputy named Kyle Dinkheller made what appeared to be a routine traffic stop. The only hint that something was amiss was the driver's failure to pull over immediately, instead choosing to proceed down a deserted side road before stopping.

Deputy Dinkheller had been in the sheriff's department for almost three years. All who knew him described him as a good officer, community oriented, a truly nice guy, prone to performing good deeds for people he barely knew.

The man stopped that day, Arthur Brannan, was a recluse, a Vietnam veteran with mental problems. On that day, he had an M-1 rifle with him in his truck. The officer's in-car camera provided both an auditory and visual record of the events that followed.

Brannan was immediately belligerent. He got out of his truck, dancing a bizarre jig in the middle of the street. At that point, realizing he had an irrational person stopped, Dinkheller radioed for assistance.

Finishing his dance, Brannan then abruptly charged the deputy. Out of camera range, there was apparently a brief scuffle, during which Dinkheller can be heard ordering Brannan back. Brannan retreated back to his truck, and, standing in the open driver's side door, pulled out the rifle, loaded it, and then leveled it at Dinkheller. For a full 10 seconds, Dinkheller repeatedly ordered Brannan to put the gun down. "He got an M-1 carbine rifle and Dinkheller was pleading with him to drop the gun when out of the blue he (Brannan) started firing," said Sheriff Kenny Webb, Dinkeller's boss ("Police Charge Man...," 1998).

Brannan's shots began a gunfight during which more than 50 rounds were exchanged. Dinkheller was wounded several times and finally collapsed on the road next to his car.

The car video shows Brannan approach the deputy and fire a fatal shot into Dinkheller's head. Brannan fled but was located the next day and arrested. He is currently serving a life sentence in Georgia for Dinkheller's murder.

Sheriff Webb and Dinkheller's fellow officers all had the same reaction on viewing the tape. Why didn't Dinkheller shoot Brannan during the more than 10 seconds that Brannan was loading his rifle and then had it leveled at the officer? It was clearly a deadly-force situation, yet Dinkheller chose not to shoot. Only after Brannan began firing did Dinkheller return fire. By that time, with Brannan's advantage of a superior weapon and a better cover situation, the outcome was ordained.

There is some evidence that Dinkheller was not unusual in his reluctance to use deadly force, even when justified. FBI studies of non-firing by law enforcement officers in the 1950s and 1960s found numerous instances of police officers, at the moment of truth, unable to use deadly force sometimes even at the cost of their own lives (Grossman, 2000).

Both police and military trainers recognize this problem and have developed training protocols to overcome it. The challenge is to assist good people to overcome their natural revulsion at harming another human being when the situation dictates. The issue needs to be addressed forthrightly in training, and some recruits may conclude they could not harm another person even in defense of themselves or others. While it is impossible to predict with certainty those who will be able to use force when necessary, those who clearly would not use force under any circumstances are not suitable candidates for policing.

Ongoing Training

All professionals require ongoing training and police officers are no exception. The legal landscape surrounding policing changes constantly, and keeping officers current with new legislation and case law requires concerted effort. The physical skills of policing, particularly use-of-force skills, are perishable, and will decline without practice. Policy changes, particularly in a sensitive area like use of force, must be reviewed, integrated as part of training, and documented.

Gordon Graham is an attorney and a captain with the California Highway Patrol. Captain Graham has developed an innovative training program that consists of six-minute training sessions at daily roll call.[1] Graham is a strong advocate of the Risk Management approach, and he conceptualizes all police activities in a matrix of high-risk (HR) activity, such as use of force, versus low-risk (LR) actions such as writing a parking tag. The other elements are high-frequency (HF) activity, such as burglar alarms, versus low-frequency (LF) activity, such as vehicle pursuits. From a risk-management perspective, low-risk activities, even when not performed frequently, are of little concern. Certain high-risk activities (e.g., responding to family trouble) are performed frequently, and thus officers develop proficiency at handling these situations. Those situations that carry the greatest risk are those low-frequency events that are high risk in nature. These HR/LF events are the ones that Graham focuses on in his six-minute roll call training program. The program is built around short scenarios that are read at roll call by a supervisor. The supervisor then leads a short discussion, with a focus on the legal and tactical issues identified in the scenario.

Graham lists several benefits to the six-minute Roll Call Training Program, but in an era of shrinking government dollars this is a program that can be implemented at very low cost. By doing six-minute training sessions daily, the average officer will be provided with an additional three days training each year at virtually no expense. Figure 8 is a Roll Call Training scenario from the Cincinnati Police Department's Roll Call Training pro-

Figure 8: Cincinnati Police Academy Roll Call Training[2]

Scenario: Poor Teamwork

It is 1500 and you are dispatched to a man with a knife on a street corner in a residential area. The dispatcher states the man is wandering on the corner with the knife in the air talking to himself. Upon your arrival you take a good tactical position keeping the patrol car between yourself and the subject. You begin isolating the situation, warning passersby back and issuing verbal commands to the subject. A backup officer arrives and decides to try and take the subject down from the rear. As the backup officer approaches, the suspect hears him and turns to him with the knife. The officer stops and turns to retreat, but trips. What do you do now?

Critical Issues:

Always think tactically. What are good contact/cover principles in this situation? What tactical options do we have? If the subject is not posing an immediate threat, is there any need to take quick action?

The scenario as described has high potential to become a deadly-force situation. Thinking legally, will you be able to articulate why any force was used or not used? Were other options available and could they have been used effectively?

Discussion:

The poor tactics of the backup officer created a lethal force situation that better tactics could have avoided. It is more than a question of simply what is legally justified. If poor tactics lead to deadly force, we may have legal justification, but we will also be held accountable for the tactics used and decisions made. Good communication among officers, good tactical sense, and effective use of available force options can minimize the necessity for lethal force.

gram which was modeled on Graham's work with the California Highway Patrol.

Police trainers face a special challenge. They have to develop professionalism that will withstand sometimes horrendous abuse. They have to instill respect for all citizens, even for those whose behavior is abusive, violent, and sometimes depraved. They must coach complex physical skills to be performed in high stress and occasionally life-threatening situations. They must train officers to respond to countless dangerous situations and not only survive but thrive under the pressure. And they must prepare officers for the possibility of inflicting pain and perhaps death on other human beings.

Discussion Questions

(1) What are the minimum training hours required for police officers in your area? Does the local department provide more than the minimum required? Do you think this training is adequate?

(2) Some police agencies are now requiring a college degree for their officers. Would you support such a requirement? Why or why not?

(3) How would you design training for use-of-force issues?

Notes

1. For more information on Graham's Roll Call Training Program, write him at Graham Research Associates, 6475 E. Pacific Coast Highway, #136, Long Beach, California, 9080, or go his website, www.gordongraham.com.

2. The scenario described is based on a situation in Philadelphia that resulted in a lawsuit against the officers and department. The shooting was

found legally justified, but the police department was found negligent for lack of training and poor tactical response.

Supervisors may want to review 12.110 Handling Mentally Ill Individuals and Potential Suicides, 12.545 Use of Force, 12.546 Taser Electronic Device, and 12.547 Use of the Bean Bag Shotguns.

Chapter 8. Steps to Minimize Police Use of Force — I

"While force is the core of the police role, the skill in policing consists in finding ways to avoid its use."

Egon Bittner (1970)

There is no shortage of suggested solutions to prevent what is generally described as the problem of excessive use of force by police. These solutions often suffer from the same lack of clarity that characterizes much of the discussion of force issues. For the most part, there is non-existent or negligible research supporting many of the proposals. Police use of force is a complex issue, and it resists the bumper sticker approach that characterizes much of our public policy.

Changes in police policy governing use of force, increased diversity in police departments, better recruiting and screening of officers, residency requirements, improved training, citizen oversight, early warning systems, community-oriented policing, and aggressive criminal and civil liability action against officers using excessive force are among some of the reforms commonly discussed. Some of these ideas have been tested, some have merit, and some represent wishful thinking. A brief review of some of these ideas will provide some clarification on what we know on the issue.

In this chapter we will discuss internal measures that police agencies can adopt to minimize the use of force. In the next chapter, we will discuss external measures involving agencies outside the police department, such as legislative bodies, courts, prosecutors and others.

Use-of-Force Policies

Does policy matter? Will officers operating under a more restrictive force policy be less likely to use force than those officers working under a broader policy? For officers in force situations, does policy influence their decision making?

Administrative policy does not exist in a vacuum. Training, supervision, and the culture of the particular department will act to inculcate the policy into officer behavior or, at the other extreme, reduce the policy to a meaningless piece of paper. A policy on use of force that is not reinforced in training, and that is ignored by supervisors, is likely worse than no policy at all since it in essence leaves force decision making entirely to the discretion of the individual officer. A carefully designed use-of-force policy reinforces agency values, describes the agency emphasis on minimizing force against citizens, provides guidance on those situations where force is appropriate, enhances officer safety, provides tactical information, and describes administrative steps in force incidents.

Policy may provide general guidance, for example, in a statement such as: "Officers are required to utilize all other reasonable options prior to using force against citizens." Policy may also be very specific, for example, containing a direct prohibition against shooting from or at moving vehicles.

Policy can go beyond the legal boundaries expressed in court decisions. While courts have emphasized the split-second nature of police force decisions, agency policy may address the officer's actions prior to the force that put the officer in harm's way and led to the use of force. Consider the officer who responds to a family trouble situation and enters a residence without a backup officer. Reacting to an attack in the residence, the officer's use of force may be reasonable. However, his decision to enter the residence alone was poor tactical decision making and could be in violation of administrative policy that requires officers, absent exigent circumstances, to wait for backup officers in potentially dangerous situations.

Policy can address specific tactical situations. Departmental policy on shooting at moving vehicles is a good example. In Boston, in September of 2002, the issue of police shooting at motor vehicles surfaced after an officer, firing shots at a vehicle which had attempted to strike him, inadvertently killed a back-seat passenger. Following the incident, Boston Police Commissioner Paul Evans proposed a change in the deadly-force policy that would prohibit officers from shooting at fleeing vehicles. The Boston Police Patrolman's Association then called for Evans to resign, stating such a policy change would endanger officers (Rivers, 2002).

Other police departments have already made this change. For example, the Cincinnati Police Department policy contains very specific guidance on shooting at moving vehicles: "Officers shall not discharge their firearms at a moving vehicle or its occupants unless the occupants are using deadly physical force against the officer or another person present, by means other than the vehicle" ("Discharging of Firearms...," 2002).

There is some research to support the notion that administrative policy can have an impact on officer behavior in force situations. In the late 1980s, Fyfe reviewed police department policies and concluded that the frequency of police use of deadly force is influenced heavily by organizational philosophies, expectations, and policies (Fyfe, 1988).

Similarly, White reviewed deadly-force data in Philadelphia following the removal of a restrictive deadly-force policy in 1974 and the reinstatement of the restrictive policy in 1980. He concluded that administrative policy can be an effective factor in controlling police use of deadly force (White, 2001).

In conclusion, it is likely that the effectiveness of administrative policy is less related to the policy itself than to the organizational context surrounding it. A use-of-force policy, no matter how elegantly crafted, that is implemented without significant organization support is unlikely to have much impact on officer behavior. Conversely, a sound policy, supported by ongoing training, enforced by effective supervision and communicated by a committed management team will not only control officer use of force but enhance officer safety and tactical practices as well.

Increasing Police Department Diversity

Skolnick and Fyfe (1993:137) state the case succinctly:

It is more difficult to treat women and ethnic minorities badly when one is sharing a patrol car with a female or minority officer. A second reason for increasing police representativeness is to introduce views and values to police ranks that may vary from those characteristic of the white males who have long dominated policing. Here, the hope is that the presumably kinder and gentler policing styles of women and nonwhite officers will rub off on the entire organization, producing a less aggressive police agency.

Are black and/or women officers really more likely to police in a "kinder and gentler" fashion than their white male counterparts? Does the available research on use of force support this notion?

On the effect of gender, a study in 1995 by Garner and his colleagues found male officers more likely to use force than female officers (Garner et al., 1995). Yet Terrill, in his large-scale observational study of police use of force, found no differences in the rate of force used between male and female officers. Terrill's study used a broad definition of force and 15.7% of the officers in his study were female. Terrill theorizes that earlier studies had too few women officers in the sample to substantiate gender differences (Terrill, 2001).

There is more research available on racial differences in officer use of force. A study of shootings by Chicago police officers found black officers more likely to shoot black citizens and white officers more likely to be involved in shooting white citizens. However, these numbers appeared to be primarily related to off-duty shootings, and probably reflected residential patterns — black officers living in black neighborhoods and white officers in white neighborhoods — as opposed to racial factors in force decision making (Geller and Karales, 1981).

A study of Ohio officers' attitudes toward use of force found that white officers were more likely to view higher levels of force as both necessary and appropriate than black or Hispanic officers (Holmes, 1997). Yet Terrill's study found "officer race had no effect on forceful behavior" (Terrill, 2001:134).

Terrill's findings are buttressed by the U.S. National Institute of Justice's use-of-force study in 1999, which stated: "Use of force appears to be unrelated to an officer's personal characteristics such as age, gender, and ethnicity" (U.S. NIJ, 1999:viii).

Diversity in American police agencies is a business necessity and is essential to the police mission. There are many benefits that accompany racial and gender diversity in policing, but the claim that diversity will have a significant impact on the incidence of police use of force is closer to wishful thinking than proven fact.

Improved Recruiting and Screening

The theory is simple enough. Cops who use excessive force are bad apples who should never have been hired as police officers in the first place. Effective recruiting and selection procedures, including screening procedures such as psychological testing, will weed these poor candidates out.

There is no doubt that recruiting police officers is an increasingly difficult proposition. In Chicago, 36,211 people signed up for the police test in 1991. By 1997, the number signing up had dropped to 10,290, and in 2000 only 5,263 people signed up for the police exam. In New York City as late as 1996, 32,000 people signed up for the police test. In 2001, less than half that number (13,136) signed up. In August of 2001, the Los Angeles Police Department cancelled an academy class because there were not enough recruits available to start the training ("Newspaper: Big City Police...," 2001).

The good economy through much of the 1990s, and the shrinking labor pool, were no doubt major factors in the declining pool of applicants. The terrorist attack of 9/11/01, and the major projected expansion of federal law enforcement, will mean increased competition for fewer candidates for local law enforcement agencies that are already struggling to replace retiring officers.

Sometimes police agencies are tempted to cut corners in recruiting. For instance, in 1980, the Miami (Florida) Police Department was ordered to immediately add 200 new officers. Negative results on background investigations and warnings by police academy staff members were ignored. As a result, "By 1988, more than a third of them had been fired. Twelve members of the group known as River Cops had been convicted of crimes ranging from drug trafficking to murder" (Delattre, 1996:8).

Similarly, in Washington DC recruiting standards and training were sacrificed to add cops in 1988 and 1989. As described by Edwin Delattre (1996:233):

> Every mistake that was made in Miami was repeated in Washington, D.C., with utterly predictable and even more disastrous results. Faced with a congressional threat to withhold $430 million unless 1,800 new officers already in residence in the city were rapidly hired, the Metropolitan Police Department hired 1,471 new officers in 1988 and 1989. Normal procedures for application were suspended in haste; and the passing grade on the entrance examination was reduced to 50 percent. Background investigations were conducted by telephone and abbreviated to the point of worthlessness; FBI criminal records checks were ignored... So trifling were the background checks that some applicants who were incarcerated at the time received letters denying them parole at the same time they were admitted to recruit classes.

A later study of Washington DC police shootings by the *Washington Post* found the recruits hired in 1988 and 1989 were involved in more than half the district's police shootings (Leen et al., 1998a).

The Rampart scandal in the Los Angeles Police Department (LAPD) provides a more recent example of the same lesson. The scandal resulted in dozens of LAPD officers leaving the department in disgrace, a payout by the city of $125 million in civil settlements, and dismissal of over 100 criminal cases poisoned by the involvement of Rampart officers. An internal review of the Rampart incident by LAPD found serious problems in the recruiting of some of the officers in the scandal. For example, pre-employment investigation of the officers had found criminal involvement, histories of violence, and narcotics activity. The report notes: "While it is impossible to substantiate completely, it appears that the application of our hiring standards was compromised when these officers were hired during periods of accelerated hiring in the late 1980s and early 1990s" (LAPD, 2000).

Accelerated hiring to bring in large numbers of new officers may be problematic even if good selection practices and hiring standards are maintained. Thus, in 1994, the City of Pittsburgh, as part of a cost-saving measure, offered early retirement incentives to officers. Between 1993 and the end of 1995, 546 officers, about 45% of the total sworn personnel, left the department. Pittsburgh then initiated a massive hiring program that by 1996 left the department with nearly half its staff as new hires. Pittsburgh's Police Chief Robert McNeilly believes many of the community problems in Pittsburgh, which led to imposition of a federal consent decree in February, 1997 stemmed from the hiring binge. Commenting on the 1993-95 exodus from the department, Chief McNeilly noted "...it was too much to lose at one time" (Davis et al., 2002:4). A Vera Institute research paper on the Pittsburgh consent decree put it more bluntly. "The new officers' inexperience led to numerous errors in judgment and performance, a situation which some community members and police personnel believe further alienated not only blacks but white members of the community as well" (ibid.).

Using psychological screening to eliminate those candidates at high risk to use excessive force is an idea that is innately appealing. The 1967 President's Commission on Law Enforcement and Administration of Justice advocated psychological testing of potential police recruits. Yet, as researchers noted almost 30 years later: "...the problem of selecting effective police officers has a much more complicated set of determinants than poor mental health and undesirable personality traits" (Grant and Grant, 1995:152). Elsewhere in their report, the researchers put it even more bluntly. "The task posed to the authors of this chapter was to look at the research evidence for links between officer selection and subsequent officer abuse of force. Unfortunately, there is virtually none" (ibid.).

There is no set of selection procedures providing a foolproof method for hiring only good police officers. The written test, long a primary element in the selection process, is of questionable validity. That is why many departments are moving to a testing process that de-emphasizes written tests in favor of assessment center-type tests that measure "job related behavior, including problem-solving ability, teamwork, communication skills, interpersonal skills, use of force, decision–making ability, ability to maintain emotional stability and to exercise good judgment under pressure" (*Community Centered Policing...*, 2001:35).

In summary, a process that includes a rigorous background investigation, plus use of polygraph and similar tests combined with psychological testing and a thorough assessment by a qualified mental health professional, would seem to offer the best odds of success.

Training

There is wide agreement that training is a key element in minimizing officer use of force. There is little argument that effective training should be realistic and scenario-based, and that it should emphasize skills to de-escalate volatile situations. Chapter 7 provided an overview of this type of use-of-force training.

The failure to provide good training can have severe consequences. A *Washington Post* report on shootings by D.C. police illuminated some of the problems subsequent to poor or non-existent firearms training. "Nearly 75 percent of the District officers who used their weapons in 1996 failed to meet the District's basic firearms standards...There have been more than 120 unintentional discharges of the gun in the past decade; 19 officers have shot themselves or other officers accidentally" (Leen et al., 1998a).

A departmental regulation requiring firearms training every six months was largely ignored. One off-duty accidental shooting resulted in a nearly $800,000 settlement against the city. In the incident, "the officer, who had not been to the firing range to qualify with his weapon for 26 months, accidentally shot and wounded his roommate" (ibid.).

Lack of training in this case extended beyond firearms training. Assistant Chief Terrance Gainer also noted deficiencies in the department's use-of-force training: "They are not being taught this (use of force) adequately. They are not practicing these skills and they are putting people at risk" (ibid.).

Recruit training, in particular, must be viewed as an opportunity to de-select those individuals who are not suitable for police work. There needs to be further discussion and research to clarify as much as possible the performance criteria for excluding individuals. Failure to eliminate poor performing recruits is a recipe for disaster. In its report on the Los Angeles Police Department, following the Rodney King incident, the Christopher Commission stated (Delattre, 1996:233):

> At present, approximately 90-95% of each entering Academy class graduates. Less than ten years ago that rate was closer to 60%. Some of this difference undoubtedly is due to changes in teaching practices, the availability of remediation programs, improvement in pre-hiring screening efforts, and reduction in physical training requirements. A portion of this change, however, seems attributable to an unwillingness to terminate poorly performing recruits, especially those protected by the consent decree or other similar mandate, for fear of civil liability or legal challenge or simply not meeting Departmental guidelines. The Commission urges that unqualified recruits not be retained for any reason. To do so only threatens the well-being of the public and the police force.

Early Warning Systems

The premise of early warning systems is that a small number of officers are disproportionately represented in use-of-force incidents. As an example, the Christopher Commission in Los Angeles found that 5% of LAPD officers accounted for 20% of reported uses of force (Walker et al., 2001). In theory, by focusing a variety of interventions on high-risk officers, a department's use of force can be reduced.

Implementation of early warning systems by police agencies is growing: "By 1999, 39% of all municipal and county law enforcement agencies that serve populations greater than 50,000 people either had an early warning system in place or were planning to implement one" (ibid., p.1). This growth seems likely to continue, especially with the 2001 Commission on Law Enforcement Accreditation (CALEA)[1] Standards that mandate an early warning system for accredited police agencies with over 300 officers.

The key issues posed by early warning systems are the types of factors to include in the system, how to weight various factors, determining the point at which an officer is "flagged" or identified through the system, and developing options for those officers identified.

CALEA lists several potential elements for use in an early warning system, including performance evaluations, citizen complaints, disciplinary actions, use-of-force incidents, internal affairs and supervisory reports, and worker's compensation claims and traffic accidents. A 2001 U.S. Department of Justice report (DOJ, 2001c) listed civil suits, use of sick leave, searches and seizures, and non-disciplinary remedial actions as other factors that might be included.

Quantifying these factors into some sort of numerical formula that would identify problem officers is a difficult challenge. For instance, compare two officers: Officer A who had five use-of-force incidents in a one-year period and Officer B who had two use-of-force incidents over the same time span. Looking more closely, we learn that Officer A works nights in a high-crime area and Officer B works days in a suburban bedroom community. Officer A had five use-of-force incidents while making 300 arrests, yet Officer B had two use-of-force incidents while making only 20 arrests. This somewhat exaggerated example illustrates the difficulty of using numerical data as the only basis for identifying problem officers through an early warning system.

Once criteria and thresholds for identifying potential problem officers are set, a process for intervening with identified officers is designed. The first step in the process is typically a meeting with the officer's supervisor and/or commander for a general review of the circumstances which led to the officer being identified by the system. It is important to remember that all of the individual incidents under consideration have already been investigated and in some cases, if appropriate, disciplinary action may have been taken against the officer. The review generated by an early warning system is in search of a pattern of events as opposed to single incidents. Consider the officer with multiple use-of-force incidents, all of which were found to be justified. The focus of the review would not be on what the officer did wrong in any one or all of the incidents, but on how these incidents might have been handled more effectively.

The outcome of this initial review could lead to a number of remedial steps, including additional training, reassignment, counseling for personal problems, or heightened supervision.

The good news is that early warning systems appear to be effective in modifying officer behavior. Researchers have studied early warning systems in three large police agencies: New Orleans, Minneapolis, and Miami-Dade County. Each of the programs was organized somewhat differently, but all reported good results. Citizen complaints against participating officers in both New Orleans and Minneapolis dropped over 60% in the year after the officers completed the program. In Miami-Dade, researchers tracked officer use of force before and after intervention through the early warning system. The percentage of Miami-Dade officers with zero use-of-force reports went from 4% to 50% after program intervention. The researchers noted: "Early warning systems appear to have a dramatic effect on reducing citizen complaints and other indicators of problematic police performance among those officers subject to intervention" (Walker et al., 2001:3).

While the focus of early warning systems is reducing officer misconduct, there are potential benefits for individual officers as well. Misconduct and poor use-of-force decisions could stem from personal problems, alcoholism, and the variety of stress-related issues that plague many police officers. The program can be designed to include referral to a variety of services designed somewhat like Employee Assistance Programs.

The major drawback of the early warning systems programs is the large administrative effort necessary to keep the program operating effectively. Particularly in large agencies, implementation and maintenance of the program requires a substantial commitment of administrative time and resources.

Community-Oriented Policing

Community-Oriented Policing (COP) is a philosophy that positions police officers as partners in an ongoing community-based effort to reduce crime and disorder. Officers work with community members to identify problems and then develop strategies to solve those problems.[2]

Robert Trojanowicz, often referred to as the father of COP, believed strongly that the new relationship between cops and communities under Community Policing would have a dramatic effect on police-community relationships. In an article detailing how COP might prevent civil disturbances, Trojanowicz (1989:12-13) provided the following specific examples of how COP could reduce tensions:

- Community Policing allows the police to gather more and better information about the level of risk in target neighborhoods.

- Community Policing provides the police with a mechanism to track incidents with racial overtones.

- Community Policing provides an important new way to address retail drug dealing, as it provides legitimacy for aggressive anti-drug initiatives by other members of the department.

- Community Policing involves residents in the police process, which improves the communication that can help defuse threatening situations.

- Community Policing allows the police to develop proactive initiatives that offer the promise of enhancing the safety and overall quality of life in the community over time.

The emphasis on problem solving as part of Community Policing provides a more concrete possibility to reduce force incidents. One example is the new approach some agencies are taking in response to mentally ill people.

Police response to violent mental patients is a high-risk event for both police and the mentally ill. In 1998, "at least 10 law enforcement officers and 37 mentally ill individuals were killed during (police) encounters. Nearly one-third of the people killed in police shootings in New York City in 1999 had mental illnesses. A review of 30 cases of people shot and killed (by police) in Seattle revealed that one-third of those shot showed signs of being emotionally disturbed or mentally ill at the time of the incident" (Johns, 2001:1).

After a fatal shooting of a mental patient in 1987, the Memphis police formed a partnership with local mental health providers to improve police response to crisis situations involving mentally ill people. A special police unit, the Crisis Intervention Team (CIT), was formed to provide intensive training on mental illness and community resources to assist ill persons. Members of the CIT respond citywide to all calls involving mental patients.

CIT appears to have had significant impact. "The program has proved highly successful in reducing officer injuries and use of force. Officer injuries during crisis calls decreased 60 percent during the first three years of the project" (*Community Centered Policing...*, 2001:55).

Similarly, in December of 2000, the Cincinnati Police Department implemented a program to improve its response to mentally ill individuals. On a pilot basis, psychiatric social workers from Cincinnati's University Hospital were assigned to work full time at one of the police department's district stations. The social workers and the officers respond as a team to calls involving mental illness. Both the social workers and the police are enthusiastic about the new working relationship, and an evaluation of the program by University of Cincinnati researchers has been funded. If the program is deemed successful, the team concept will be implemented throughout the city.

Systematic study and analysis of force incidents may provide insight into the nature of the locations and types of calls where officers are at high risk of being involved in a force incident. Understanding of these situations may lead to better tactics or problem-solving approaches that reduce risks at a particular location.

COP, with its emphasis on developing relationships with community people, appears to hold some promise in reducing the violence between community people and the police. Perhaps its primary promise is the potential to mitigate the effects of high-profile incidents on police-community relationships. In theory, where the relationship between the police and community is solid, that relationship will weather the stress of individual incidents and defuse the tension that accompanies use-of-force incidents.

Discussion Questions

(1) Compare use-of-force polices from two or more police departments. What common elements do you find? Do you believe these policies provide adequate guidance to officers in the field? How would you strengthen them?

(2) Review the process used by a local department in selecting police officers. How would you evaluate the effectiveness of the screening process?

(3) How much influence do you believe a police chief has in controlling use of force by his or her officers? To what extent should police chiefs be held accountable for excessive use of force by members of their departments?

Notes

1. The Commission on Accreditation for Law Enforcement Agencies, Inc. (CALEA), was established as an independent accrediting authority in 1979 by the four major law enforcement membership associations: International Association of Chiefs of Police (IACP); National Organization of Black Law Enforcement Executives (NOBLE); National Sheriffs' Association (NSA); and Police Executive Research Forum (PERF).

2. For an introduction to COP, see: Howard Rahtz (2002). *Community Policing: A Handbook for Beat Cops and Supervisors.* Monsey, NY: Criminal Justice Press.

Chapter 9. Steps to Minimize Police Use of Force — II

> *"But the public, the media, and numerous powerful opinion-shapers would find some of their convenient assumptions about the police challenged by a greater familiarity with the facts."*
>
> William Bratton and Chuck Wexler
> *And Justice for All*, 1995

In the last chapter, we reviewed measures that police agencies can adopt internally to reduce the use of force. In this chapter, we continue the discussion by evaluating measures to control use of force that require the intervention of one or more non-police agencies.

Residency Requirements

Supporters of a residency requirement claim it will have an impact on police officer performance. The belief is that "Residency requirements and incentives affirm the connection between officers and the communities they serve" (*Community Centered Policing...*, p.37).

To maximize the supposed benefits of residency, some cities provide financial incentives for officers to live not just in the city proper but in high-crime areas within the city. One example is Atlantic City, NJ, which "has tailored its officer home loan program to provide a strong incentive — the lowest interest rates and the fewest number of years for loan forgiveness — for residency in the most disadvantaged areas of the city" (ibid., p.42).

Philadelphia has taken the residency requirement a step further. The city now mandates that appointment as a Philadelphia police officer requires city residency for one year *prior* to appointment. The net effect of this rule will be to greatly restrict the number of applicants from outside Philadelphia.

Research on the impact of residency requirements on police behavior provides little guidance. A New York State government report in 1985 noted a perception among African Americans and Hispanics that police were more likely to use deadly force against minorities. The report listed several recommendations tailored to change that perception, including residency requirements (Condon, 1985). A 1980 study found that community perception was indeed influenced by residency requirements, noting a positive correlation between residency and the tendency of community members to rate police services as "outstanding." Yet the same study found that residency requirements had negligible effect on the attitude of officers toward community members (Smith, 1980).

The belief that residence in the jurisdiction in which the officer serves will have a positive impact on officer performance has a certain logic and appeal. Tying residency to officer performance is a more difficult proposition. How a police officer performs is a function of a large number of variables that may or may not include residency. At this point, evidence that residency requirements have any significant impact on police officer performance is, at best, inconclusive.

Citizen Review

Historically, police departments have policed themselves through internal affairs units and investigations. Behind the cry for citizen review is the increasingly common belief that the police cannot be trusted to police themselves.

Civilian review of the police is a relatively recent phenomenon. The history of civilian review boards dates only to the 1960s, but with dramatic growth during the 1990s. A report in 1994 found that citizen review programs had increased 74% between 1990 and 1994 (Walker and Knight, 1994).

Police have generally been resistant to civilian review. In the 1960s, critics of police review were fond of quoting J. Edgar Hoover's statement that the boards would have the effect of "paralyzing the police." A National Fraternal Order of Police publication from the same era claimed that a proposed review board in New York "exudes the obnoxious odor of communism" (Skolnick and Fyfe, 1993:219). Yet police in some jurisdictions where citizen review is in place have learned to live with it, if not embrace it.

The major concern police have about citizen review is the belief that those without police experience cannot possibly understand the intricacies and complexity of the situations cops are forced to deal with. This concern of the police is often derided as an indication of a cover-up mentality, the oft-referred to "Blue Curtain" or "Blue Wall of Silence." Yet by wanting to restrict this review to their peers, police are not unlike other professions. Lawyers make a particularly interesting comparison as they are often in the forefront of efforts to implement citizen review. Thus, Perez and Ker Muir (1995:215) note: "It is not irrelevant to the police that the legal profession's own internal disciplinary mechanism seldom finds fault with attorneys accused of misconduct. Early research revealed that in only slightly more than one percent of the cases which it investigates did the bar's own grievance handling committee find fault with its peers."

There are a number of issues involved in the establishment of a citizen review board. The first and likely most contentious issue is whether the newly created entity will be an investigative body separate from the police or a review-only body without investigative responsibilities.

The City of Berkeley, California has a citizen review board (the Berkeley Police Review Commission or P.R.C.) that has been in operation for over 20 years. The Berkeley commission has its own civilian investigators, directly accepts citizen complaints at its own intake location, and reports its findings directly to the Berkeley city manager. Minneapolis, San Francisco, and Washington, D.C. are three other cities that have elected to establish civilian run investigative bodies outside the police department (*Community Centered Policing...*, 2001).

Portland, Oregon provides an example of an auditing type of citizen review. The Portland Internal Investigations Auditing

Committee (PIIAC) is composed of city council members, neighborhood representatives appointed by the mayor, and at-large representatives appointed by council members. The PIIAC function is to "hear appeals from citizens dissatisfied with police investigations of their complaints, review all closed cases involving allegations of the use of excessive force, and conduct random audits of internal affairs investigations" (ibid.).

Kansas City takes a civilian monitor approach that utilizes the ombudsman model. The Office of Civilian Complaints, the O.C.C., takes citizen complaints and forwards them to the Kansas City Police Department's Internal Affairs Unit. Completed investigations on the complaints are sent back to O.C.C. "Internal Affairs in Kansas City does not recommend possible investigation outcomes or disciplinary action. Only evidence, statements, and investigation summaries are included in I.A. files. After the O.C.C. staff approves a complaint investigation, it formulates a recommendation regarding the case. The O.C.C. process is then complete, and the investigation is referred to the chief of police" (ibid.).

In the rare times when the Kansas City Police Chief does not agree with O.C.C. recommendations, "...the chief and director of O.C.C. meet. Both the chief and director indicate that when such a meeting occurs, agreement is normally reached after brief discussion" (ibid.).

Implementation of civilian review can take several paths, and one of the first issues is appointment and selection of members. In Florida, the Miami-Dade County Independent Review Panel (IRP), has nine members. Five community groups[1] are allocated slots, with four additional members selected by the IRP panel. The community groups each provide a list of three candidates from which the county commissioners choose one. The Portland PIAAC includes a mix of neighborhood association representatives, city council appointees, and two members selected by the police commissioner.

The Rochester Police Department in New York is an agency that provides ongoing training and consultation for review board members (Finn, 2000:24):

In Rochester, New York, candidates for the review board attend a condensed version of a police academy run by the police department. The 48-hour course involves 3 hours per evening for 2 weeks and 2 all-day sessions. The members use a shoot/don't shoot simulator, practice handcuffing, and learn about department policies and procedures, including the use-of-force continuum.

The expectation that citizen review will have significant impact on police behavior or citizen satisfaction with the police is not supported by the facts. The belief that police misconduct is widely ignored or minimized by police internal investigations is contradicted by research findings that: "Everywhere else that parallel outcomes have been tracked for civilian and internal review, the internal system has been more prone to find police misconduct" (Perez and Ker Muir, 1995:210). The lone exception found was Berkeley. In the early 1990s, the review board found officers guilty of misconduct in 17% of the cases, compared to the Berkeley police internal system, which found officers guilty 15.7% of the time, a small difference (ibid.).

Will those citizens who actually complain about the police be more satisfied with a civilianized complaint process? The evidence suggests otherwise. "Most complainants reject the legitimacy of any sort of police review system, no matter how 'fair' it may appear to be, because they usually lose their cases" (ibid.). Commenting on this trend, Skolnick and Fyfe (1993:219) note: "The reason why is that most citizens' allegations cannot be definitively resolved one way or the other. It is often a 'he said, she said' situation with few if any non-biased witnesses."

Poorly designed and organized review bodies may have a negative influence on police-community relations. The Washington, DC Civilian Complaint Review Board, disbanded in 1995, developed a tremendous backlog of cases that left both complainants and police officers frustrated. A review body that fails to control the scope of its work risks irrelevance. Findings released years after the incident, long after the officer may have been exonerated or disciplined through the police internal process, only serve to reinforce the notion of citizen review as inept, inefficient, and a waste of government resources.

The Berkeley Police Review Commission, the most comprehensive review panel in the country, basically duplicates the police complaint and internal investigations process. In a large jurisdiction, this is an expensive undertaking and raises questions about efficient use of tax dollars. The auditor model used in Portland and Kansas City may provide a more fiscally efficient model that accomplishes the purpose of external review and community accountability without creating a duplicate (civilian) investigatory and review system.

Civil Liability Action against Officers

Civil suits filed against the police have skyrocketed over the last 30 years. In 1967, there were 1,741 cases filed against the police. By 1971, the number of cases filed yearly had jumped to 3,894. Five years later, in 1976, 13,500 cases were filed, a number that doubled again by 1982. There are now an estimated 30,000 lawsuits filed annually against police officers (Ross, 2001).

Most civil suits are resolved without going to trial, and police cases are no exception. Some jurisdictions routinely hand out large amounts in settlements and judgments. For example, a review of police-related suits in Washington, DC found the city paying out $1 million per year in settlements and judgments (Horwitz, 1998).

In theory, civil suits can act as a "catalyst for change" in a number of ways. Mary Cheh (1995:235) suggests:

...damage awards can spur reform if the costs of misbehavior are high. Civil law suits permit broad discovery of information and may provide a means to uncover police misbehavior and stir public reaction. Finally the civil law offers various possibilities for framing relief which go beyond punishment or compensation and include remediation. That is, the civil law offers equitable relief, via court injunction and specific orders, that can force a deficient department not only to pay for harm caused but to reform so that the harm is not likely to be repeated.

Are payments to complainants in civil suits likely to have any impact on the level of use of force by police? There is some belief that these suits can modify police behavior by highlighting procedural problems or training issues. Thus, Walker and his colleagues (2001) recommend that civil litigation against officers has a place as an indicator in Early Warning Systems. And the U.S. Department of Justice, in its review of the Cincinnati Police Department, recommended that Police Academy staff be briefed on all civil suit settlements for possible use in training (DOJ, 2001b:14).

There is no clear evidence that the financial costs associated with civil suits have any impact on police behavior. However, the belief is that by penalizing government for police misconduct (through financial settlements), governmental leaders will force policy and other changes on the police.

While a single substantial award could bankrupt a small jurisdiction, for large jurisdictions, despite increasing damage awards, the amounts paid out in civil suits constitute only a minute percentage of the overall government budget. They may be viewed by some officials as simply a cost of doing business. Consider that in Los Angeles, "even if half of the LAPD's $11.3 million liability bill in 1990 could be eliminated and converted to police salaries and personnel expenses, it would pay for only about seventy officers, less than a 1 percent increase in the department's personnel complement" (Skolnick and Fyfe, 1993:207).

The idea that training and policy changes may emanate from review of individual liability suits ignores the fact that civil suits are generally filed well after the incident in question. Since the overwhelming majority of the settlements come years after the incident has been reviewed and investigated, the odds are low of new insights stemming from the suit.

That said, civil action offers perhaps the most effective redress for individuals and their families who have been affected by questionable use-of-force incidents. The analogy is to medical or other professional malpractice. If a police officer makes a misjudgment in a use-of-force incident, that is a professional error for which an injured person should have some legal remedy.

Accordingly, a 1999 study by the National Academy of Sciences estimated that between 44,000 and 98,000 people die annually due to mistakes by medical professionals. And some experts believe that somewhat astounding number is conservative. "That's probably an underestimate for two reasons," noted Dr. Donald Berwick of the Institute of Medicine (CNN.com, 1999):

> One is, there are many different kinds of errors we never learn about — even in retrospective studies — because they are never written down. And second, these studies did not include other areas of care like home care, nursing homes and ambulatory care centers.

The general reaction by victims and their families to these medical mistakes is to sue. Civil action against the people responsible is the widely accepted response. Criminal prosecution, in any but the most egregious cases, is not pursued. In fact, Skolnick and Fyfe (1993:198) note "even when the evidence in civil actions demonstrates with some certainty that professional wrongdoing also has involved criminal violations, prosecutors usually keep their distance."

Is the comparison of deaths stemming from police action (mistakes?) to deaths arising from medical mistakes a valid one? Certainly there is a qualitative difference. Deaths resulting from police intervention stem from violent, sometimes public and high-profile incidents. The death is unexpected and shocking to family members and friends of the victim.

Medical mistakes occur in a sheltered environment at the hands of people who are assumed to be compassionate caregivers and whose motives are above question. Yet from a civil liability point of view, both may be errors resulting not from malice or purposeful maltreatment but from a professional decision that with the luxury of hindsight proves faulty.

Criminal Prosecution of Officers

Criminal prosecutions of officers stemming from force incidents are unusual. A 12-year study of police shootings by Los Angeles County Sheriff's Deputies found 477 shooting incidents but only one criminal prosecution. In that case, a deputy was sentenced to eight months in jail "after falsely reporting a disturbance at a ...home in 1982 to justify a raid there. After kicking in the door, he shot Delois Young, 22, who was holding an unloaded rifle. Young survived, but her 8-month old fetus was killed" (Geller and Scott, 1992:292).

Even in those cases that appear to most observers to clearly involve excessive force, juries are reluctant to convict police officers. The Rodney King incident — in which Los Angeles police officers were charged with assaulting King — provides a notable example. The day after the jury came in with a not guilty verdict, "a poll conducted for USA Today poll found 86% of whites and 100% of blacks agreeing that 'the verdict was wrong.' Most of the national news magazines conducted polls in the same time period and reached similar results" (ibid., p.51).

One problem is that the criminal law and its sanctions are a blunt instrument largely unsuited for judging the complexity of force incidents. The law itself provides officers with tremendous latitude in force situations, asking only that the officer act in a "reasonable" manner. And citizens are generally reluctant to impose criminal guilt on a cop "just doing his job." Cheh notes: "Jurors are naturally sympathetic toward an officer, who, after all, became involved in the incident as part of his duties. They are reluctant to brand him a criminal and find beyond a reasonable doubt that he committed a crime. Contrariwise they usually see the victim as unsympathetic, as contributing to the event, or as a criminal who deserved what he got" (Cheh, 1995:243).

However, as in the Rodney King case, exoneration on state charges may not be the end of the story. Federal criminal civil rights charges may follow, especially in high-profile incidents. Yet the conviction rate in civil rights cases is also very low. In 1990, of almost 8,000 cases forwarded for review to the U.S. Department of Justice, indictments were returned in 30 cases and convictions obtained in 18 (ibid., p.246). Some of the same dynamics likely are similar to those operating in state criminal trials.

There is also concern among police officers that political considerations are a major factor in prosecutorial decisions, particularly in high-profile incidents. Michael Stone, a police defense specialist, notes: "These agencies (for example, the United States Department of Justice, state departments of justice, and county prosecutors) have demonstrated that their efforts in this area are driven, at times and in part, by political or public opinion considerations. More than one case in this writer's personal experience has resulted in an indictment or trial, following public outrage and interest group influence at the highest levels of prosecutorial policymaking and discretionary decision making" (Stone, 2002a:4).

Nevertheless, criminal prosecution of police misconduct, including excessive use of force, is an appropriate tool for individual incidents that rise to the level of criminal conduct. As has been noted elsewhere, serious police use of force is statistically a relatively rare event. And within this subset, incidents of clearly excessive force that could be judged criminal are rarer yet. As a tool to hold individual officers accountable for their criminal conduct, whether force-related or not, prosecution is clearly appropriate. As a tool to somehow modify or reduce overall use of force by police officers, criminal prosecution of individual officers seems unlikely to have much impact.

"Patterns and Practices" Suits by the Department of Justice

A provision in the 1994 federal Omnibus Crime Act authorized the U.S. Attorney General to bring civil action against local governments engaging in patterns and practices of police conduct that deprive citizens of their constitutional rights. Using the authority granted under this law, the Department of Justice (DOJ), has instituted what are referred to as "patterns and practices" investigations in several local jurisdictions across the country. These investigations have resulted in consent decrees in Los Angeles, California; Washington, DC; Pittsburgh, Pennsylvania; and Steubenville, Ohio. The consent decrees are court-negotiated agreements that dictate changes in police policy, training, and other agency operations.

Pittsburgh was one of the first "patterns and practices" cases initiated by the DOJ under the 1994 law. In 1996, the Pittsburgh ACLU brought a class action suit against the city claiming a pattern of civil rights violations by city police officers. In April of 1996, the DOJ initiated its investigation, and in January 1997 a

DOJ letter to city officials alleged a pattern of excessive force, false arrests, improper searches, poor disciplinary practices, and an organizational failure to supervise police officers.

Initially, city officials reacted with frustration and disbelief. They expressed the feeling that Pittsburgh had been targeted unjustly, and the mayor, police chief, and city lawyers all decided to fight the allegations in court. But over the next few months, city officials changed their minds and agreed to a settlement with the DOJ and imposition of consent decree. The city and DOJ signed the consent decree in April of 1997. Under the consent decree, the city was required to make significant changes in operation of the police department (Davis et al., 2002:7):

> The settlement outlined specific policy and practice changes that the city had to comply with. It instructed the Bureau of Police to make comprehensive changes in oversight, training, and supervision of officers. Among the key elements was a requirement that the Bureau develop a computerized early warning system to track individual officers' behavior; document uses of force, traffic stops, and searches; and provide annual training in cultural diversity, integrity and ethics. The decree also required changes in the processing of citizen complaints, including liberalized filing procedures and more thorough investigations.[2]

An evaluation of changes in policing as a result of the consent decree in Pittsburgh was completed by the Vera Institute of Justice in 2002. The report states: "It is irrefutable that the consent decree has led to many positive changes in Pittsburgh policing" (ibid., p.62). The report notes specific improvements procedures related to use of force, searches, citizen complaints and traffic stops. Improved training is noted, especially officer training on use of force.

The Vera study did not report specifically on changes in the incidence of use of force by Pittsburgh officers since imposition of the consent decree. The study did note that both police supervisors and officers believed "...that officers were hesitant to conduct searches and use force since the consent decree was signed. Of course, care in conducting searches and in the use of force was one of the goals of the decree. But officers and supervisors told us that officers, afraid to use force, were taking extra time to react, putting themselves in danger...Injury to officers because they are afraid to use appropriate force is a significant source of contention between the union and the administration" (ibid., p.51).

While the Vera study did not provide any statistical data documenting changes in use-of-force incidents, they did review changes in community perception on police use of force. These findings were mixed. "Overall, 34% of people felt the police used excessive force less often than five years ago. This compares to 29% who felt things had stayed the same, and 27% who thought things had become worse. African-Americans were...more pessimistic than whites as to whether change had taken place: 43% of African-Americans thought abuse of force was more common, compared to only 13% of whites" (ibid., p.39).

On February 3, 2003, U.S. District Court Judge Robert Cindrich granted a joint motion filed by the City of Pittsburgh and the DOJ to terminate the 1997 consent decree, citing substantial compliance by the City of Pittsburgh with the decree provisions.

The Collaborative Agreement in Cincinnati

Following the riots in Cincinnati in 2001, Mayor Charles Luken requested a DOJ patterns and practices investigation of the Cincinnati Police. The DOJ and the city eventually signed a Memorandum of Understanding agreeing to changes in police department practices that were similar to those mandated under consent decrees in Pittsburgh and other cities. However, the DOJ agreement in Cincinnati was overshadowed by a unique "collaborative settlement" negotiated in federal court. This settlement began with a suit filed in March of 2001 against the city in federal court. The suit, alleging racial profiling by Cincinnati police, was a cooperative action between the local American Civil Liberties Union (ACLU) affiliate and a Cincinnati-based organization, Black United Front (BUF). In May, after the riots, city council voted to accept mediation of the suit, and federal Judge Susan Dlott appointed a "special master" to mediate the suit. Chosen to mediate the suit was Jay Rothman, an attorney with a firm, the Aria Group, that specializes in conflict resolution. Rothman and the Aria group had experience in mediating conflicts around the world, including Bosnia, South Africa, Sri Lanka and the Middle East. Parties to the settlement effort included the ACLU, BUF, the City of Cincinnati, and the local Fraternal Order of Police (FOP).

Rothman initiated a series of meetings with various groups of stakeholders: city employees, police officers and their families, black citizen groups, white citizen groups, and other minority groups. Each group made detailed lists of recommendations to improve both policing and police-community relations in Cincinnati. The representatives of each group met and distilled the recommendations down to an agreed upon set of ideas that formed the basis of the settlement. Key points in the agreement were establishment of a new Citizen Complaint Authority, changes in use-of-force policy and reporting, a commitment to Community Problem-Oriented Policing by the Cincinnati Police Department, and a commitment by both the city and community members to work together on community problem solving. After a year of turmoil, an agreement among groups including the FOP, ACLU, and Black United Front was nothing less than astounding. As Mayor Luken put it, "It's historic. At the risk of sounding sensational, it's an unprecedented turning point for the city" (Goetz and Korte, 2002).

SUMMARY

The wide variety of suggested remedies to reduce police use of force is a testament to the complexity of the problem.

Where officers are engaged in criminal conduct, whether in a force-related incident or not, they must be held accountable just as any other citizen. The New York City police officers who sodomized Abner Louima with a toilet plunger committed an act of unspeakable brutality, and even the most rabid police supporters in the country would agree those responsible deserve harsh punishment for that criminal behavior. But critics who attempt to portray every police force incident with the brush of Rodney King or Abner Louima do no one a favor by their gross oversimplification of the issue.

The overwhelming majority of police force incidents involve officers making their best professional judgment, under stress, in a time frame of seconds or less. In hindsight, we can review the officers' tactics, training, and the force decisions made with the goal of improvement where necessary.

What should be the response to those incidents where the officer made a misjudgment? Where there was clearly no criminal intent by the officer, civil action represents the most appropriate venue for individuals harmed by police mistakes. Police, no less than doctors, make errors in high pressure situations where people's lives are at stake. The civil arena is the place to attempt to remedy these errors.

Yet both these strategies are designed for individual incidents, and their impact on overall police use of force, unless it results in a landmark case like Tennessee v. Garner, is minimal at best. Increasing use of civil litigation against officers in use-of-force cases probably enriches attorneys more than it affects police behavior.

Civilian oversight organizations charged with independent investigation and/or the review of police force incidents are an increasingly prevalent part of the policing landscape. The bottom line of these organizations, whatever particular powers they are granted, is to provide some external audit and review of police activities, particularly uses of force. Yet historically, the police internal investigations process treats officers more harshly than outside civilian authorities. Research simply does not provide support for the notion that civilian oversight will have an impact on either police behavior or on citizen satisfaction with a civilianized complaint process. But judging the concept of civilian oversight simply on this basis is short-sighted.

Ask any cop if he believes the Internal Revenue Service, the Environmental Protection Agency, or any other governmental group should be subject to ongoing monitoring and review by external bodies. The overwhelming majority of officers, like other informed citizens, recognize the importance of outside review to ensure agency integrity and compliance with the rules. Yet many of the same officers who would scoff at the idea of the IRS or another government entity policing itself strongly oppose any sort of civilian oversight of police operations.

Police power and authority are unmatched by any other government entity. This fact argues for more oversight, not less. Unfortunately, many of the civilian oversight programs of the past have been marked by incompetence, or were politically-driven, and their performance as investigatory agencies has been in some cases pathetic. Supporters will argue that structural problems such as lack of funding, poorly defined mandates, and weak understanding of policing have been at the root of their problems. In many cases, this was undoubtedly true.

Nevertheless, strong and effective civilian oversight can enhance police credibility and effectiveness in the community. Police managers have a stake in strong and effective civilian review because properly designed external review adds to police legitimacy in the community and assists in fulfillment of the police mission.

Early warning systems have demonstrated a clear ability to reduce use-of-force incidents by "high-risk" officers identified in these programs. If properly structured, these programs can directly benefit officers and enhance police agency operation. Effective early warning systems require strong administrative effort and monitoring, and a major commitment of department resources. Recently developed computer software can ease the burden of the operation of these programs.

The long-term impact of the involvement of the federal government on local policing has yet to be determined. Review of the consent decrees signed between the Department of Justice and various cities reveals a similar set of changes imposed. In many instances, it appears that mandates in one city have been simply cut and pasted into the agreements of others. The real issue is how these agreements will affect officer behavior on the street. The challenge for researchers is to monitor the variety of policy, training, and operational changes that have been instituted, and then to track their effectiveness. The Vera study of the 1997 DOJ mandated changes in Pittsburgh found mixed results, but judged the

Pittsburgh police improved in many areas. In 2003, the federal court agreed, and the Pittsburgh consent decree was terminated.

The recently signed settlement in Cincinnati provides a fertile opportunity for learning. This agreement represents a shared vision of what policing should be, according to a consensus among citizens, neighborhood leaders, elected officials and police officers. It also makes neighborhood leaders responsible and accountable for the problems in their neighborhood, and commits all to a shared process of community problem solving. Whether the potential embodied in the agreement is realized only time will tell.

Discussion Questions

(1) Does your local police department have a civilian oversight program? Describe its structure and authority. How are citizens chosen to serve? How would you describe its effectiveness?

(2) Have you ever made a citizen complaint about a police officer? Describe your experience.

(3) Do drug dealers and others sometimes use citizen complaints to harass officers? How would you address this problem?

(4) Review a consent decree signed by the DOJ and a city. These may be found on the DOJ website, www.usdoj.gov. Pick out one of the recommendations and critique it.

Notes

1. The five groups with seats on the IRP panel are the Community Relations Board; the Community Action Agency; the League of Women Voters; the local bar association; and the Miami-Dade Police Chief's Association.

2. Copies of the consent decrees signed by various cities are available from the DOJ website: www.usdoj.gov.

Chapter 10. When the Worst Happens

"When it ended, the youth was dead of a gunshot wound to the chest — and the city was in turmoil."

Barry Horstman (2002)

"The death of someone related to a police activity, instantly triggers the interest of a variety of agencies, systems, and groups, each with its own focus, perspective, and point of view."

Michael Stone (2002b)

The police are called to a domestic disturbance. A father and his teenage son are fighting. When the cops arrive, the argument escalates. Stories about what happened next vary. The police claim the son attacked them with a knife. Family members insist there was no reason to shoot and they call it murder.

Word spreads on the street. Groups of people gather on corners to hear the news. Rumors spread through the crowds: "White cops killed him." "They shot him in the back for no reason." "The cops shot him 13 times." "The cops were laughing."

Police responding to calls in the neighborhood are rocked and bottled. Reporters at the scene interview relatives and friends of the victim. The family members are distraught. "The cops are supposed to protect us," the father cries, "not kill us." Friends begin to create a makeshift memorial outside the house, spray painting area buildings with remembrances of the victim and anti-police slogans. The news media report ongoing complaints of police harassment of citizens that have been ignored by the city, and further violence is predicted.

The next day a crowd gathers at city hall demanding answers. Police officials are tight-lipped, stating the incident is under investigation and refusing to make any further comment. The officers involved are put on administrative leave. Some politicians and community leaders demand the cops be fired and that federal authorities investigate the incident. The cops cannot be trusted to investigate themselves, they say.

Within a few days, the history of each cop involved is rehashed in the media. One of them is a rookie, and the radio talk show speculation is that he was scared and overreacted, shooting when there was no need. An older officer involved has a disciplinary history, and was once suspended for arguing with a supervisor. He also has had several citizen complaints against him and was involved in previous force incidents. News reports suggest that this is perhaps a bad cop.

The day of the funeral is particularly tense. Reporters reveal rumors of threats against the police. The police clear the streets for the funeral procession, but otherwise keep a low profile.

Over the next weeks, the family files a civil suit against the city, the officers involved, and the police chief. There are news reports on the training that police receive and comments from citizens complaining that the cops are impersonal, rude, and do not respect the people in the community. The role of internal investigations is examined, highlighted by statistics showing how rarely citizen complaints result in the disciplining of officers.

A few weeks later, the local prosecutor issues a finding that the police acted lawfully, in self-defense. The family is outraged, but profess they are not surprised. It's pretty much what they expected, since the cops always cover for each other. They want a federal investigation, and political leaders again request that the Department of Justice and the FBI investigate the shooting incident.

Community leaders say the problem is bigger than bad cops. It's a lack of jobs, poor housing, and ineffective schools. They demand more funds for social service programs to attack what they describe as the underlying problems in the neighborhood.

Almost a year after the incident, the police department's internal investigation concludes that the officers made tactical errors, and they receive written reprimands. The family's attorney holds a press conference. "A man is gunned down," he says, "and the cops get a written reprimand. So much for justice."

Time goes by. The police come and go, and the relationship between cops and residents settles into an uneasy truce until the next major incident.

After a police shooting or force incident, variations on this story are played out in cities and towns across the country. A police shooting or major force incident has consequences not only for the victim and his family and friends, and the police officers involved, but for the life of the community as well.

Impact on the Victim's Family

Most of us can only imagine the emotional pain in losing a loved one to violence. The suddenness of the death, the utter senselessness of the situation, and the physical disfigurement and suffering of the victims all heighten the intensity of the reaction to a violent death. When the police are responsible for the death, these feelings may be further escalated.

The process of the death investigation, as it does for the officer, will tend to intensify the frustration and anger felt by family members. Details of the event may be sketchy, and the police are likely to be reluctant to release details while the investigation is ongoing. Witnesses and friends may report a version of the incident that is dramatically different from the official reports. The body of the victim will be held for investigation and an autopsy, a step which may be interpreted as further depersonalization of the victim. Media reports may paint the victim in an unflattering light, highlighting criminal behavior as an example. In addition to the emotional toll, the death may bring additional financial and legal burdens to the family.

For the victim's loved ones — as for the involved police officer — the circumstances of the incident are likely to be the most important factor in their reaction. But community response, emotional support systems available, and individual psychological makeup will all play a role in reaction to the event.

In incidents where victims are unarmed, are involved in minor crimes, are teenagers rather than adults, and where it appears as if the police use of deadly force was mistaken or excessive, the emotional reaction is likely to be heightened.

Impact on the Officer

For a police officer, "the use of deadly force can be the beginning of a nightmare that never ends" (Burson, 2001:4). Officer reaction to a deadly-force event will vary widely depending on the circumstances of the event itself; prior training and experience; department, community and legal reaction; support systems available to the officer; and individual officer characteristics.

While different researchers have provided varying descriptions of the process, officers involved in these incidents typically go through four identifiable stages.

The first stage is reaction during the incident itself. The majority of officers report perceptual distortion, a sense that time slows down; the incident seems to occur in slow motion. Hearing and vision are affected. The officer may report hearing sounds that didn't occur. Auditory exclusion, the failure to hear sounds, is common. Visual effects, a vivid sense of detail, and tunnel vision are also widely reported.

During the incident, a chemical soup of hormones is released into the bloodstream. These chemicals, most notably endorphins and norepinephrine, have important physiological consequences.

Norepinephrine is a by-product of adrenaline and acts to "enhance alertness and efficient problem-solving" (ibid., p.9). Endorphins are natural painkillers that represent biological preparation for survival. However, another consequence of high levels of endorphins is "poor memory and possible amnesiac states" (ibid., p.10). This endorphin overload is one possible explanation for the failure of victims of traumatic events to remember details of the incident.

In the second stage, the initial aftermath of an incident, an officer may feel shock and disbelief. He may experience "shock symptoms such as tremors, shaking, crying, nausea, hyperventilation, and so on" (Solomon, 2002:2). Immediately after an incident, the officer may be dazed and have trouble grasping the reality of what just occurred. The officer may find it "difficult to concentrate and to remember details" (ibid.).

The third phase, what Burson calls the "afterburn" period, can last up to three days. Burson believes: "This is a serious time for the officer, and is also the time where intervention can minimize the effects of the trauma" (Burson, 2001:6).

During this period, it is common for officers to experience sleeplessness, nightmares, flashbacks, and generalized anxiety. The officer may attempt to self-medicate these feelings with alcohol or other drugs. Media reports of the incident, often distorted and inaccurate, combined with the officer's and the department's inability and/or unwillingness to respond, may lead to a sense of helplessness; this contributes to the officer's viewing himself as a victim of events over which he has no control. The process of the investigation of the incident itself may also act to inflame the officer's anxiety.

The officer's spiritual life is tested. He may have taken another human being's life. There may be anger at the victim for having forced the officer to take a life. The officer may engage himself in critical questioning of his own actions, a "what-if" process that increases the officer's anger and sense of helplessness in the situation. One author has reported a "strong impulse to resign from the police department, probably in an attempt to escape from the events surrounding the incident" (Jones, 1989:29).

In dealing with his peers after the event, the officer can be confronted with what Jones refers to as "Locker Room Shock." In an attempt to be supportive, fellow officers may "suggest that the officer should have shot the suspect several more times, or may congratulate him on 'being a man.' Officers seldom find comfort in such comments" (ibid.).

In the weeks and months that follow an event, a number of officers may begin showing symptoms of Post Traumatic Stress

Disorder (PTSD). Not every officer involved in an incident will experience a traumatic reaction. Solomon (2002:1) estimates, "About one-third have a mild reaction, one-third have a moderate reaction, and one-third have a severe reaction." Effective recognition and treatment of PTSD is the key to a return to emotional health for the officer.

Community Effects

The community reaction to a deadly-force incident will vary from indifference to civil disorder. Circumstances of the incident, racial differences between officers and victims, political and media reaction, and the state of community-police relations will all factor into potential reaction. For police managers, these incidents pose a clear threat to the organization. Officer morale, discipline, and public confidence are all at risk in the department's handling of these events.

For political leaders, the failure to respond effectively can have drastic consequences, including civil disorder, flight of residents and business interests, and the loss of citizen faith in government.

Reviews of deadly-force incidents and community responses have identified predictable "flash points" (U.S. DOJ, 2002). At each of these critical points following a deadly-force incident, police and community leaders can take steps to minimize the chances that an incident will become a catalyst for community disorder and division.

The initial flash point is the governmental response immediately following the incident. In the hours following the incident, officials should emphasize the investigative process that will occur. Unsubstantiated judgments on the appropriateness of the police action should be withheld, and derogatory comments about the victim — disclosure of his criminal or drug history as an example — should be avoided. An expression of condolence to the family, personally delivered if possible, will also act to reduce tension. Release of available information about the incident to the media may assist in quelling rumors.

Force incidents may generate protest marches and rallies that have the potential to escalate into disorder. Police officials in these situations walk a tightrope in organizing a police presence and response that provides for community safety and freedom of expression without appearing provocative or repressive to protest participants. Dialogue and joint planning with protest organizers can help ensure that these events do not degenerate into civil disorder.

Information about the process of the investigation into the incident should be fully explained to family members, community leaders, and the media. At any point in the process where the results of the investigation are to be publicly disclosed, a briefing to family members and community leaders prior to the public release should be arranged.

If an incident results in a trial or court action, planning for the aftermath of a verdict by police and community leaders should be carried out beforehand. When a court decision is imminent, notification of officials of the pending action can ensure that the necessary resources are in place.

Balancing Act

A deadly-force incident is first and foremost a potential criminal incident, and it must be investigated with the same tenacity and professional thoroughness as any major offense. From the police point of view, the investigation itself must take priority. This does not mean that the primacy of the investigation allows the department to run roughshod over any concerns for the officers involved. Nor does it mean that the department can escape any involvement or responsibility for notifying family members of the incident in a timely and concerned fashion. And it certainly doesn't mean the department can turn a blind eye to the short- and long-term consequences of the incident in the community. It does mean that the department must handle all the above carefully, balancing the rights and interests of all the parties.

Most police departments recognize the potential for damage to officers involved in these incidents. Within the limitations of the investigation, the officer should be treated with compassion and concern. At the scene, a supervisor should be assigned to stay with the involved officer(s). The role of this supervisor is to act as a calming and reassuring presence. The supervisor may explain to the officer the process of the investigation and assist the officer in contacting his or her family members to assure them the officer's well-being. The supervisor also assures that the officer makes no statement except to the assigned investigators. Some departments have peer support programs allowing other officers who've been involved in shootings to provide emotional support to the involved officers.

Many departments have a policy of removing involved officers from street duty following a shooting or major force incident. Making this a mandatory policy removes its punitive nature, especially if it is stressed to the officer and the community that this is a routine step and not a comment on the officer's conduct. A visit to a police psychologist or counselor during the days immediately following an incident will provide the officer an opportunity for emotional release, as well as education on the stress-related symptoms he may be experiencing.

There is probably not a more difficult job in the world than to tell someone a family member has died. This is a job that very often falls to police officers. When the death is a result of police action, the issue of how to do the death notification is doubly difficult. Circumstances will sometimes outrace plans in these incidents. Relatives will hear of the death from others long before any official notification can be completed. Family members may show up at the crime scene demanding to see the body, striking out verbally and sometimes physically at the police. In these instances, police leaders have to adapt to the situation by maintaining a concerned and helpful demeanor.

When time permits, the notification can be done in a fashion that respects the grief of the family and reinforces the department's integrity and professionalism. While the notification is a police responsibility, that responsibility can be appropriately shared. Clergy, social workers, and neighborhood leaders may all be members of a notification team. The strong physical reaction to such tragic news can be life-threatening and some cities have an ambulance on standby while the notification is made (Smith, 2001).

After the initial notification, family members should be kept informed of the progress of the incident investigation. If the family is hostile to the authorities, a third party can be recruited to act as a link between the police and the family.

Community reaction may be dependent, in part, on media coverage of the incident. In the aftermath of an incident, there is tremendous pressure on police and political leaders to make statements about the case. This pressure becomes increasingly intense when the failure to comment directly on the case is interpreted by the media and others as evidence that something must be wrong. One suggestion in these circumstances is to talk about the nature of the investigation, departmental standards for use of force and department training in use of force. Initial statements must balance the integrity of the investigation with the department's emphasis on accountability. Statements can acknowledge the feelings and concerns of the family and friends of the victims and at the same time recognize the concerns of the officers involved and their family members. Captain Greg Meyer, a use-of-force expert with the Los Angeles Police Department, provides the following example of wording that accomplishes this goal (Stone, 2002b:7):

> I realize this a controversial incident and we are committed to re-solving it. It is understandable that the friends and families in-volved are highly concerned about what has happened. The con-cerned families include those of the involved civilians and the of-ficers themselves.

News media coverage of a controversial police use-of-force incident may reflect the ongoing relationship between the local media and the police as much as the facts of the incident. In the best of times, police-media relationships are uneasy. For the public to be well informed is always in the best interest of the police, and the media are the major source of public information. If the police department's only effort at community education is in reaction to crisis, the message may well be lost. Media people who understand use-of-force issues are more likely to provide objective coverage of force incidents.

Lessons Learned

In February of 2003, a Cincinnati police officer responding to a burglar alarm at a business witnessed a man exiting through the broken front window of the business. The officer pursued the suspect on foot, catching up with him in an alley. There was a physical struggle, during which the suspect tore the PR-24 baton from the officer's belt and began hitting the officer in the head with it. The officer then fired several shots, killing the suspect.

The officer was white, the suspect African American. With the memories of the rioting in April of 2001 still fresh, the city held its collective breath. The shooting was the first since the heavily publicized Collaborative Agreement was reached in April of 2002, and many people viewed the shooting as the first test of that agreement.

Within a few hours of the shooting, city officials, including the mayor, visited family members of the deceased to express condolences. A press conference was called to quickly provide what information was available to the public. Community activists were notified and briefed on the incident, and even escorted through the crime scene after the initial investigation was completed. The level of openness was very deliberate. Greg Baker, head of the Police Relations Unit of the Cincinnati Police Department, described the actions as, "...just good business" (Wood, 2003).

The handling of the incident by police and city officials was given much credit for keeping the city calm. The *Cincinnati Post*, commenting on the changed atmosphere in the city, editorialized: "And that is in no small part a testament to the lessons learned by city and police officials over the past two years" ("Learning...," 2003).

SUMMARY

Planning for the aftermath of a controversial force incident can mitigate the impact on all parties. Training for officers on the impact of involvement in force incidents is crucial. Peer support and other programs can cushion the physical and psychological stress arising from these incidents, and reduce the risk of PTSD. An investigative protocol that recognizes the impact of the incident on the officer's memory, as well as protecting the legal rights of involved officers, should be established. Procedures for handling death notifications should be in place, and appropriate clergy and others committed to assisting should be ready and able to respond on short notice. Training and rehearsal for these situations must be provided. Police leaders must ensure ongoing education of community and media leaders on use-of-force policy and training. And planning for incidents should be comprehensive and continuous.

Managing of all the competing interests in a fashion that effectively shields the integrity of the investigation, protects the officer's rights, and maintains public confidence in the police department and local government is a challenge for the best of leaders.

Discussion Questions

    (1) How would you describe the police-media relationship in your jurisdiction? Give specific examples.

    (2) What steps would you suggest that police leaders take immediately following an incident?

    (3) Review some news articles on police shootings. Do you think they treated the officers fairly? How was the victim of the police shooting portrayed?

    (4) Are there any preventive steps that community leaders can take to reduce the chance of civil disorder following a questionable use-of-force incident?

Chapter 11. Toward a Better Understanding

"The significant problems we face cannot be solved at the same level of thinking we were at when we created them."

Albert Einstein, quoted in
7 Habits of Highly Effective People, by Stephen Covey

For most police officers, the threat is never really out of mind. Not the threat of serious injury or even death as a result of performing a dangerous job. That is a threat that was understood when the officer signed up. But the even bigger concern, the nightmare that haunts police officers, is the possibility of a mistake, shooting the wrong person, making a misjudgment that cost another his life. Every police officer in the country understood when Sean Carroll, a New York City Police Department officer, began to weep when he turned over the body of Amadou Diallo and found not a gun, but a wallet.

In the storm of publicity that follows a high profile use-of-force incident, it is easy to lose track of a few basic facts. Despite the television and movie image, police rarely use force. As noted in chapter 2, only about 1% of people who had face-to-face contact with the police reported the officers either threatened or used force. The majority of the force was low level, pushing or grabbing, with firearms used in only two of every 10,000 arrests. And deadly force by police has steadily declined over the past 25 years.

Despite the low numbers, force situations involve such high risk for involved officers, citizens, and communities that every step possible to minimize use of force should be taken. There is no panacea, no single policy change or new technology that will accomplish this. But there are some areas where improvements can be accomplished.

New Technology

The ultimate police weapon, a device like the "phaser" used in Star Trek, remains the province of science fiction. Most of the tools available to police officers are literally "stone-age" in their application. The strikes and kicks taught as defensive tactics to police officers are not radically different from the fighting techniques human beings have been engaged in since they were running from dinosaurs. The police nightstick, despite its transition from wood to metal, and its new nomenclature as an "impact weapon," remains a metal stick not much different from that used by our earliest ancestors to whack each other over the head. The technology of firearms is literally hundreds of years old and though undeniable advancements have been made, the basic principles of guns as a weapon remain the same.

Two technological advances that stand out are chemical irritant and the Taser. The evidence on the chemical irritant is convincing. It works most of the time, can allow the officer to maintain some distance from a suspect, and reduces both officer and suspect injuries. Any agency not providing chemical irritant as a force tool for its officers is needlessly putting its own officers and citizens in jeopardy.

The Taser, or electronic "stun gun" as it is more popularly known, is a weapon that begins to fulfill the potential of technology for controlling aggressive and disorderly individuals. But there are a high percentage of tactical situations where the Taser falls short of its promise. Its effective range is limited; it is difficult to use on a person not standing relatively still; and heavy clothing will defeat the electrical current the Taser uses to immobilize people.

Force technology and development of less-than-lethal alternatives will not come without controversy. Police agencies will be reluctant to deploy less-than-lethal alternatives without strong assurances they will, in fact, work. Thus, after a high profile police shooting in England, the Home Office approved of the use of "stun guns" by British Constables. David Blunkett, the Home Secretary, proposed using the Tasers "to give police a "third way" between using batons or guns (Kamel and Thompson, 2001). The idea has drawn a cool reception, with only one city, Northhamptonshire, choosing to purchase the Tasers. The resistance to deploying the Tasers was explained by Roger Gray, an author and police firearms instructor: "If we start complicating the thought processes of the officers involved, innocent bystanders are going to end up hurt or killed. You can't walk into a situation with a Batman utility belt of options and then decide on a scale of one to ten which is the most appropriate" (ibid.).

Some groups will object to the use of new force technology on the somewhat curious grounds that it does not work with guaranteed effectiveness. In Philadelphia, police used a stun gun to subdue a man who was naked and threatening people with a knife. The officers first attempted to use pepper spray, but the man was not affected. The police then successfully utilized the Taser. However, the man died on the way to the hospital. Although the man had cocaine in his system and the autopsy results were pending, some groups called for an immediate ban on police use of the Tasers. The ACLU and Amnesty International "called on law enforcement and correctional agencies to suspend use of the weapons (Tasers) until an independent inquiry can be completed" (Loviglio, 2001). The call to ban the Tasers ignores that fact they are often used in deadly-force situations. Removing the Tasers means leaving police with firearms as their only option.

Research and development of non-lethal options needs to be accelerated. Captain Greg Meyer, a use-of-force expert with the Los Angeles Police Department, put the challenge eloquently when he asked: "If we can put a man on the moon and return him safely to Earth, why can't we put a man on the ground and take him safely to jail?" (Meyer, 1993).

National Data Collection

The federal Violent Crime Control and Law Enforcement Act of 1994 required the Attorney General to "acquire data about the use of excessive force by law enforcement officers" and to "publish an annual summary of the data acquired..." (McEwen, 1996a:vii).

The effort to collect such data is hampered by several obstacles. Getting 17,000 police departments to agree on force definitions and a national reporting system will take a level of cooperation between local and federal government rarely seen. But the failure to do so will continue a system of fragmented and incomplete information providing a national picture of police use of force with a questionable relationship to reality. The federal government originally funded the International Association of Chiefs of Police (IACP) to collect data on use of force. The IACP provided very broad definitions of force and asked law enforcement agencies to voluntarily provide data. IACP created an automated reporting system that allowed police departments to provide data on use of anonymously. The project lasted five years, and though project software was provided to over 4,000 police departments, the number of departments participating never got beyond 200 annually. Still, the final report of the project, *Police Use of Force in America 2001* (IACP, 2001), is likely one of the most comprehensive collections of data on police use of force available.

In 1993, Antony Pate and Lorie Fridell, in a report for the Police Foundation (Pate and Fridell, 1993), suggested a systemic and standardized method for defining and reporting police use of force. While the IACP project was a step forward, comprehensive and standardized reporting of police use of force is not much more developed than it was in 1993.

Policy and Training

For those police agencies seeking an outside review of its policy and practices, the most logical option is the accreditation process developed by the Commission on Accreditation of Law Enforcement Agencies (CALEA). The CALEA standards cover every aspect of the organization, including its policy and training on use of force. Meeting CALEA standards is an intensive and time-consuming process, but it demonstrates a high level of professionalism in agency operations. Unfortunately, CALEA standards do not provide much specific guidance on use-of-force issues. They require a use-of-force policy, regular training on the weapons issued to officers, and a reporting system for use-of-force incidents. But the standards are silent on the specifics of good policy, training content, and appropriate reporting practices.

Another option, generally much less pleasant and much more expensive, is to be the subject of a Department of Justice "patterns and practices" investigation. The end result of these investigations may be loss of local control through the imposition of a consent decree or memorandum of agreement that mandates policy and training changes. The loss of control is certainly an issue, but the expense associated with implementation of DOJ-funded mandates can be a significant burden on the local government. For example, in Pittsburgh the cost of implementing just one of the mandates, the early warning system, was $1 million (Davis et al., 2002). The initial cost of the DOJ settlement with Cincinnati in 2002 was listed as $12.5 million, but it has significantly increased since that first estimate ("U.S. Provides...," 2002).

There seems to be room for a third alternative. As use of force is the one area that generates the most controversy, there would appear to be a need for a voluntary evaluation process that could be provided by an independent consulting body. Limiting the process to use of force would minimize the administrative burden. And having a non-punitive inspection process conducted by an outside agency could be seen as an investment to forestall the expense associated with DOJ entanglement. Perhaps the federal government could even provide some financial support to agencies seeking such an evaluation or directly fund an organization such as the Police Executive Research Forum (PERF) or the IACP to provide the service.

The Race Divide

In addressing the divide between police and minorities, particularly African Americans, the police start with a substantial reservoir of goodwill. A DOJ survey of public attitudes toward the police in 12 major cities "found 80% of Americans satisfied with the police in their communities. Not only are 90 percent of whites satisfied, but 76 percent of black Americans report being satisfied with their local police" (Walker, 2000:2-3).

While the difference in the satisfaction rate between whites and blacks illustrates the racial divide, the 76% rating by blacks would be the envy of almost any other institution. Similar polls regarding satisfaction with other institutions have found rankings that included: organized religion, 25%; the military, 44%; Congress, 12%; and the press, 14% (ibid.).

The ongoing discussion of racial profiling should go beyond the statistics. Studies on profiling to date have been largely inconclusive, but the debate on the issue is likely to intensify. Race-based data collection efforts are now part of the policing landscape, particularly in urban areas. Conflicting conclusions drawn from these efforts will no doubt continue to be the focus of heated debate.

The particular facts of the issue may be of little interest to the African American who believes, rightly or wrongly, that his traffic stop was the result of profiling. An exchange at a 2001 conference at Illinois University on racial profiling captures the dilemma.

A speaker at the conference, Heather MacDonald of the Manhattan Institute and the author of an article "The Myth of Racial Profiling" (2001), referred to the issue of racial profiling as "conceptually incoherent and statistically bogus." To prove racial profiling exists, she said, people turn to anecdotal evidence and she noted: "People's descriptions of their experiences with the police can vary from the truth." MacDonald suggested "police departments directly address the minority perception that they are the target of discriminatory policing" (Erford and Zeman, 2001).

MacDonald's comments drew quick response. "Audience member Joe Price, deputy chief of the Illinois Attorney General's Chicago office, stood and said, 'Racial profiling exists. Driving while black exists.' When MacDonald asked how he could be so certain, Price responded, 'By being a black male in law enforcement for 32 years'" (ibid.).

Most police managers recognize the crucial nature of good community relations and support efforts to bring the community and police together. Ride-a-long programs and Citizen Police Academies are two widely used programs. A concerted effort to bring African Americans into these programs would pay long-term dividends.

Involving the African-American community in discussions about use of force, citizen complaints, and police training will help to close the gap in understanding that threatens the underpinnings of our community life. This dialogue can be started through churches, civic groups, and universities. Given the history shared by police and African Americans, these may not always be friendly discussions. The fact that this dialogue is likely to be difficult makes it no less important.

The community also has a responsibility. Desiree Cooper, a columnist with the *Detroit Free Press*, put it nicely: "Just as the community accuses the police of profiling minorities, the community is guilty of 'profiling' the police. Not all police are corrupt just because a few are. Not all police are quick with the trigger. Not all are disrespectful to law-abiding citizens" (Scoville, 2000:8).

For Police Managers

Officer safety concerns are at the root of a lot of the sleepless nights that haunt police executives. We provide the best equipment the department can afford, emphasize good tactical practices, and provide training, policies, and supervision all designed to minimize the risks our officers face. Yet the area that is sometimes ignored as an officer safety factor is the relationship that exists between the police and the people in the communities they serve. Particularly in neighborhoods plagued by crime, drugs, and disorder, police are under constant pressure to take action. We organize arrest sweeps, do jump-outs on street corners, utilize aggressive stop-and-frisk tactics, and confiscate impressive quantities of drugs and guns. Particularly in those communities where the relationship between the police and the people in the neighborhood is tense, officers sometimes begin to view themselves as in a war zone, surrounded by hostiles. The language that surrounds drug enforcement, the "war on drugs" rhetoric, reinforces this perception. Without clear strategic thinking, we risk winning the daily street battles but losing the long-term war.

Community policing and problem solving offer an alternative. These are strategies that emphasize results, safer communities, rather than the unending recording of drugs confiscated and arrests made. These strategies require partnerships in the community, but offer the long-term promise of success that the enforcement-only approach has never delivered. They also offer the hope of a relationship between the police and community where officer safety is enhanced and use of force is minimized. Oakland police officer Derrick Norfleet described to John Burris the promise of community policing. "Changing stereotypes, breaking down myths, and reintroducing police as individuals, as people who happen to keep law and order in your neighborhood. Our presence should be comforting rather than confrontational or hostile" (Burris, 2000:202).

And for Police Officers

Policing is the most difficult and complex profession there is. It is not likely to grow easier in the near future. The decline in violent crime enjoyed through the 90s is apparently over, and homicide rates in several cities have jumped since 2000. A recent study by the U.S. Bureau of Justice found felons "more likely to be armed than they were a decade ago, are carrying more powerful weapons and are more willing to use them" ("Felons Increase...," 2001).

At the same time, the public expectations of police are growing. In 1973, 73% of Americans responded affirmatively when asked: "Are there any situations you can imagine in which you would approve of a policeman striking an adult male citizen?" Yet by 2000, only 64% of Americans responded affirmatively to the same question. Thus, there are a significant number of Americans who apparently believe police officers are not entitled to use force even when being attacked. The same study found 10% of Americans disapproving of an officer striking a citizen who was actively attacking the police officer (Felton, 2002).

Police are thrust into situations that demand the wisdom of Solomon but without time to consider the alternatives. The decisions police make, particularly use-of-force decisions, reflect no-win situations, and regardless of the outcome some people will be unhappy.

In this age of political correctness, police officers are about the last group people feel free to stereotype and make generalizations about. Let one officer make a racist statement and we're all bigots. Let an officer use excessive force and we're all Nazis. Let an officer allow his emotions to get the best of him or use profanity, and we're all mean-spirited and lack professionalism.

There are some individuals on this job who have no business carrying a badge and a gun. There are officers out there whose behavior makes good cops cringe. It is our responsibility as professionals to rein them in, and if they cannot change, we need to get rid of them.

Being a police officer is an awesome responsibility. A friend of mine used to decry "costume wearers," people in police uniforms with little appreciation for the heart that good policing requires. If you can't handle that responsibility it is time to find another line of work.

The bottom line is that each of us is accountable for the fashion in which we deal with our fellow human beings. Brutality and excessive force have no place in professional policing. The departments and citizens that employ us expect us to perform with both compassion and competence. We should accept no less from each other.

Selected Resources

For Further Reading:

1. Burris, J. (2000). *Blue vs. Black: Let's End the Conflict Between Cops and Minorities*. New York, NY: St. Martin's Press.

2. Faulkner, S.D. (1999). *Use of Force: Decision Making and Legal Precedence*. London, OH: Ohio Peace Officer Training Commission.

3. Geller, W. and H. Toch (eds). (1995). *And Justice for All: Understanding and Controlling Police Abuse of Force*. Washington, DC: Police Executive Research Forum.

4. Geller, W. and M. Scott (1992). *Deadly Force: What We Know*. Washington, DC: Police Executive Research Forum.

5. Grossman, D. (1996). *On Killing: The Psychological Cost of Learning to Kill in War and Society*. New York, NY: Little, Brown, and Co.

6. Kennedy, R. (ed.), (1997). *Race, Crime and the Law*. New York, NY: Pantheon Books.

7. McEwen, T. (1996). *National Data Collection on Police Use of Force*. Washington, DC: U.S. Department of Justice and National Institute of Justice.

8. Skolnick, J.H. and J.J. Fyfe (1993). *Above the Law: Police and the Excessive Use of Force*. New York, NY: The Free Press.

9. Terrill, W. (2001). *Police Coercion: Application of the Force Continuum*. New York, NY: LFB Scholarly Publishing.

10. Thompson, G. (1983). *Verbal Judo: Words for Street Survival*. Springfield, IL: Charles Thomas.

11. PolicyLink in Partnership with the Advancement Project (2001). *Community Centered Policing: Force for Change*. New York, NY: author.

12. Brown, J.M. and P.A. Langan (2001). *Policing and Homicide, 1976-98: Justifiable Homicide by Police, Police Officers Murdered by Felons.* Washington, DC: U.S. Bureau of Justice Statistics (March).

Useful Websites:

1. www.killology.com/art

   This is the website of Dave Grossman, author of *On Killing: The Psychological Cost of Learning To Kill in War and Society* and *Stop Teaching Our Kids To Kill: A Call to Action Against TV, Movie and Video Game Violence.*

   The website has several articles of interest covering the effects of stress on physical performance and the training of police officers.

2. www.ojp.usdoj.gov/bjs

   This is the website of the Bureau of Justice Statistics. It contains publications on a wide variety of criminal justice related topics including use-of-force data.

3. www.usdoj.gov

   This is the homepage of the U.S. Department of Justice. It is a link to a variety of government publications including copies of the DOJ Consent Decrees signed with various cities.

4. www.policeone.com

   This site contains a daily compilation of news stories on policing from around the world. There are special links for police officers.

5. www.vera.org

   This is the site of the Vera Institute of Justice, a non-profit organization devoted to criminal justice issues. The institute has opened a link related to the Police Monitor, a position which oversees the consent decrees and agreements between the Department of Justice and various cities across the country.

6. www.policylink.org

This is the website of the PolicyLink group, a non-profit group dedicated to building strong communities. Their report, *Community-Centered Policing* (2001), contains a wealth of material on community-police relations. The report is available on their website.

7. www.calea.org

The Commission on Accreditation for Law Enforcement Agencies, Inc. (CALEA), was established as an independent accrediting authority in 1979 by the four major law enforcement membership associations: International Association of Chiefs of Police (IACP); National Organization of Black Law Enforcement Executives (NOBLE); National Sheriffs' Association (NSA); and Police Executive Research Forum (PERF).

8. www.policeforum.org

The Police Executive Research Forum (PERF) is a national membership organization of progressive police executives from the largest city, county and state law enforcement agencies. PERF is dedicated to improving policing and advancing professionalism through research and involvement in public policy debate. A variety of publications and educational opportunities are available through PERF.

9. www.theiacp.org

The International Association of Chiefs of Police is the world's oldest and largest non-profit membership organization of police executives, with over 19,000 members in over 100 different countries. IACP's leadership consists of the operating chief executives of international, federal, state and local agencies of all sizes. The IACP reports on use of force as well as other research documents are available on the site.

10. www.aslet.org

ASLET is the American Society of Law Enforcement Trainers. ASLET is dedicated to enhancing and promoting excellence in law enforcement training, while increasing the effectiveness of its members to better serve their communities and society.

References

"Accused of Excessive Force, Officers Reinstated" (2001). AP Roundup, *Law & Order Newswatch*, July 11.

Adams, K. (1995). "Measuring the Prevalence of Police Abuse of Force." In: W.A. Geller and H. Toch (eds.), *And Justice for All: Understanding and Controlling Police Abuse of Force*. Washington, DC: Police Executive Research Forum.

Alpert, G. and M. Smith (1999). "Police Use-of-Force Data: Where We Are and Where We Should be Going." *Police Quarterly* 2(1):57-78.

Anderson v. Russell (2001). 4th Circuit Court, Opinion No. 001406.P.

Binder, A. and L. Fridell (1986). "Lethal Force as a Police Response." *Criminal Justice Abstracts* (June):250-280.

Biram, J.D. (2002). Presentation in Columbus, Ohio on February 1, 2002 by the Training Director of the Missouri State Police.

Bittner, E. (1970). *The Functions of Police in a Modern Society*. Cambridge, MA: Oelgeschlager, Gunn & Hain.

"Black Leaders Back Police Commissioner; Union Sticks to Demand for Resignation" (2002). *PoliceOne.com*. (Accessed September 29, 2002.)

Bratton, W. (1998). *Turnaround*. New York, NY: Random House.

Brown, J.M. and P.A. Langan (2001). *Policing and Homicide, 1976-98: Justifiable Homicide by Police, Police Officers Murdered by Felons*. Washington DC: U.S. Bureau of Justice Statistics.

Burris, J. (2000). *Blue vs. Black: Let's End the Conflict Between Cops and Minorities*. New York, NY: St. Martin's Press.

Burson, D. (2001). "Critical Incidents: Management's Role." An unpublished paper written for Northwestern School of Police Command and Staff, Evanston, IL.

California Commission on Peace Officer Training and Standards (2001). "Training and Testing Specifications for Peace Officer Basic Courses." Sacramento, CA.

Cheh, M.M. (1995). "Are Law Suits an Answer to Police Brutality?" In: W. Geller and H. Toch (eds.), *And Justice for All: Understanding and Controlling Police Abuse of Force.* Washington, DC: Police Executive Research Forum.

CNN.com (1999). "Medical Errors Kill Tens of Thousands Annually, Panel Says." November 30. (Accessed 4/13/02.)

Commission on Accreditation of Law Enforcement Agencies (CALEA), (1999)."Standards for Law Enforcement Agencies." In: *The Standards Manual of the Law Enforcement Agency Accreditation Program,* 4th ed., standard 1.3.1.

Common Sense for Drug Policy (2001). "New Jersey Troopers Accept Plea Bargain, Avoid Jail; Case Helped Spark Nationwide Debate Over Profiling." (www.csdp.org/news).

Community Centered Policing: Force for Change (2001). New York, NY: PolicyLink in Partnership with the Advancement Project.

Condon, R. (1985). "Report to Governor Mario M. Cuomo: Police Use of Deadly Force in New York State." Albany, NY: New York State Division of Criminal Justice Services.

Daley, R. (1988). *Man with a Gun.* New York, NY: Simon and Schuster.

Davis, R., C. Ortiz, N. Henderson, J. Miller and M. Massie (2002). *Turning Necessity into Virtue: Pittsburgh's Experience with a Federal Consent Decree.* New York, NY: Vera Institute.

Delattre, E.J. (1996). *Character and Cops: Ethics in Policing.* Washington, DC: AEI Press.

"Discharging of Firearms by Police Personnel" (2002). *Cincinnati Police Procedure Manual,* P.M. 12.550, 9/2/02.

"DOJ Data on 19M Stops Finds No Profiling" (2002). *Crime Control Digest* 36(16), April 19:1.

Edwards, S.J., J. Granfield and J. Onnen (1997). "Evaluation of Pepper Spray." (NIJ Research in Brief Series.) Washington, DC: U.S. Department of Justice.

Erford, B. and E. Zeman (2001). "Illinois Police Discuss Racial Profiling." *The Daily Illini* website: www.dailyillini.com. (Accessed July 20, 2001.) [Also called the Daily Illini On-line.]

Faulkner, S.D. (1999). *Use of Force: Decision Making and Legal Precedence*. London, OH: Ohio Peace Officer Training Commission.

"Felons Increase Use of Guns; More Likely To Fire Than A Decade Ago" (2001). *Crime Control Digest* 35(45), November 9.

Felton, B. (2002). "The Real Facts about Force." *American Police Beat* IX(4) (May):1.

Finn, P. (2000). "Getting Along with Citizen Oversight." *FBI Law Enforcement Bulletin* 69(8)(August):22-27.

Fyfe, J. (1988). "Police Use of Deadly Force: Research and Reform." *Justice Quarterly* 5(2):165-205.

Gajdostik, M. (2001). "Training Feature: Improving Control Techniques." *PoliceOne.com*, June 28.

Garner, J.H., T. Schade, J. Hepburn and J. Buchanon (1995). "Measuring the Continuum of Force Used by and against the Police." *Criminal Justice Review* 20(2):146-168.

Gates, H.L. (1997) "Thirteen Ways of Looking at a Black Man." In: R. Kennedy (ed.), *Race, Crime and the Law*. New York, NY: Pantheon Books.

Geller, W. and H. Toch (eds.), (1995). *And Justice for All: Understanding and Controlling Police Abuse of Force*. Washington, DC: Police Executive Research Forum.

—— and M. Scott (1992). *Deadly Force: What We Know*. Washington, DC: Police Executive Research Forum.

—— and K. Karales (1981). "Split-second Decisions: Shootings of and by Chicago Police." Chicago, IL: Chicago Law Enforcement Study Group.

Goetz, K. and G. Korte (2002). "Deals Provide 'Turning Point.'" *Cincinnati Enquirer*, April 4.

Gordon, R. (1995). "'Cowboy' Cop at Scene of Violence." *San Francisco Examiner*, June 9.

Graham v. Connor, 490 U.S. 386 (1989).

Grant, D.J. and J. Grant (1995). "Officer Selection and the Prevention of Abuse of Force." In: W. Geller and H. Toch (eds.), *And Justice for All: Police and the Excessive Use of Force.* Washington, DC: Police Executive Research Forum.

Grossman, D. "Psychological Effects of Combat." In: *Encyclopedia of Violence, Peace and Conflict.* St. Louis, MO: Academic Press. (www.killology.com/art).

Hall, J. (1992). "Constitutional Constraints on the Use of Force." *FBI Law Enforcement Bulletin,* 61(2)(February):22-31.

Hanson, R. (2001). "Krupinski Innocent of Manslaughter." *The Detroit News*, August 10.

Harris, D.A. (1999). "The Stories, the Statistics, and the Law: Why 'Driving While Black' Matters." *Minnesota Law Review* 84(2)(December):269.

Holbrook, T. (2001). "Marchers Urge Police Review by Civilians." *The Courier-Journal*, June 11.

Holmes, S. (1997). "Defining the Occupational Definition of Police Use of Excessive Force." Doctoral dissertation, the University of Cincinnati.

Horn, D. (2001). "Civility Turned to Anarchy: How It Happened." *The Cincinnati Enquirer*, April 16.

Horstman, B. (2002). "St Pete's Shooting, Riots, Foreshadowed Cincinnati's." *Cincinnati Post*, April 10.

Horwitz, S. (1998). "When Officers Go Too Far." *The Washington Post*, November 19.

International Association of Chiefs of Police (IACP), (2001). *Police Use of Force in America 2001*. Gaithersburg, MD: author.

Jacobs, D. and R. O'Brien (1998). "The Determinants of Deadly Force: A Structural Analysis of Police Violence." *American Journal of Sociology* 103(4):837-862.

Johns, T. (2001). "Responding to Individuals with Mental Illness." Unpublished paper written for the Southern Police Institute, December.

Jones, C.E. (1989). *After the Smoke Clears: Surviving the Police Shooting: An Analysis of the Post Officer-Involved Shooting Trauma*. Springfield, IL: Charles Thomas.

Jones, T. (2001). "Electronic Immobilization Devices." *Law Enforcement Technology* (October):70-75.

Kamel, A. and T. Thompson (2001). "Police To Be Armed with Stun Guns." *The Observer* (United Kingdom), July 15.

Kennedy, R. (ed.), (1997). *Race, Crime and the Law*. New York, NY: Pantheon Books.

Klockars, C. (1995). "A Theory of Excessive Force and Control." In: W.A. Geller and H. Toch (eds.), *And Justice for All: Understanding and Controlling Police Abuse of Force*. Washington, DC: Police Executive Research Forum.

Kocieniewski, D. and R. Hanley (2000). "An Inside Story of Racial Bias and Denial: Files Reveal Drama Behind Profiling." *NY Times On-Line*, December 3, (www.nytimes.com).

Lamberth, J. (1996). *Wilkins v. Maryland State Police*, (No. MJG-93-468). Testimony from plaintiff's expert.

Langan, P., L. Greenfeld, D. Smith, S. Matthew and D. Levin (2001). "Contacts between Police and the Public." Washington, DC: U.S. Department of Justice.

"LAPD Hit Again" (2000). *This Week in Law Enforcement,* 1(16):5, December 25.

"Learning from our Mistakes" (2003). Editorial, *The Cincinnati Post*, February 11.

Leen, J., J. Craven, D. Jackson and S. Horwitz (1998a). "D.C. Police Lead Nation in Shootings: Lack of Training, Supervision Implicated as Key Factors," *Washington Post*, November 15.

—— J. Craven, D. Jackson and S. Horwitz (1998b). "New Recruits, and a New Weapon." *Washington Post*, November 18, 1998.

—— and S. Horwitz (1998). "Armed and Unready: City Pays for Failure To Train Officers With Sophisticated Weapon." *The Washington Post*, November 18, p.A-1.

"Less-Lethal" (2001). *Law Enforcement Technology* (October):62-69.

Locke, H.G. (1995). "The Color of Law and the Issue of Color: Race and the Abuse of Police Power." In: W. Geller and H. Toch (eds.), *And Justice for All: Understanding and Controlling Police Abuse of Force*. Washington, DC: Police Executive Research Forum.

Los Angeles Police Department (2000). "Rampart Corruption Incident, Executive Summary." Los Angeles, CA.

Loviglio, J. (2002). "Stun Guns Safety Issues Raised." *Associated Press*, February 16.

MacDonald, H. (2001). "The Myth of Profiling." *City Journal* 11(2) (Spring):14-27.

—— (2000). "How to Train Cops." *City Journal* (Manhattan Institute), 10(4)(Autumn):46-61.

—— (1999). "Diallo Truth, Diallo Falsehood." *City Journal* 9(2)(Summer):12-28.

Malley v. Briggs, 475 U.S. 335, 341, 89 L. Ed. 2d 272, 106 S. Cot. 1092, 1986.

McCaffery, K. (2001). "Using Persuasion Tactics to Manage Conflict." *Police Magazine* 25(1)(January):26.

McEwen, T. (1996a). *Executive Summary, National Data Collection on Police Use of Force*. Washington, DC: U.S. National Institute of Justice.

—— (1996b). *National Data Collection on Police Use of Force.* Washington, DC: U.S. Department of Justice and National Institute of Justice.

Meyer, G. (1993). "Brutal by Default: The Police Need More Humane Ways to Subdue Resisting Suspects." *Los Angeles Daily Journal,* August 19.

"Minneapolis Mayor Seeks Calm After Boy, 10, Hit by Police Bullet" (2002). *PoliceOne.com,* August 24.

Monadnock Police Training Council, Inc. (1998). "Monadnock Baton Chart." Fitzwilliam, NH.

Moore, R.F. (2002). "Citizen Panel: No Inquiry on Killing." *Charlotte Observer,* February 27.

"Newspaper: Big-City Police Depts. Facing Personnel Crisis" (2001). *This Week in Law Enforcement,* 2(29), August 6.

New York State Attorney General's Office, Civil Right Bureau, (1999). "The New York City Police Department's 'Stop and Frisk' Practices: A Report to the People From the State of New York, Office of the Attorney General." New York, NY.

Nowicki, E. (2001a). "Body Language." *Law and Order* 99(8)(August):25-28.

—— (2001b). "Expandable Batons." *Law and Order* (December):24-27.

Ohio Peace Officer Training Commission (2000). "Basic Peace Officer Training Program." Columbus, OH.

Oregonian (The), (1995). Editorial, May 5.

Pate, A. and L. Fridell (1993). *Police Use of Force: Official Reports, Citizen Complaints, and Legal Consequences.* Washington, DC: Police Foundation.

"PD To Check Applicants For Bias — Providence" (2001). AP Roundup, *Law & Order Newswatch,* June 7.

Perez, D.W and W. Ker Muir (1995). "Administrative Review of Alleged Police Brutality." In: W. Geller and H. Toch (eds.), *And Justice for All: Understanding and Controlling Police*

Abuse of Force. Washington, DC: Police Executive Research Forum.

Pinizzotto, A. and E. Davis (1999). "Offenders' Perceptual Shorthand: What Messages are Law Enforcement Officers Sending to Offenders?" *FBI Law Enforcement Bulletin* 68(6)(June):1-6.

Plakas v. Drinski, 19 F. 3rd 1143 (7th Cir. 1994).

"Police Announce Changes After Café Raid" (2001). AP Regional Roundup, *Law & Order Newswatch*, June 28.

"Police Charge Man with Killing Deputy" (1998). Associated Press report in the *Augusta Chronicle*, January 12.

Rivers, E.F. (2002). "Statement of Black Religious Leaders: On Recent Shootings and in Support of Law and Order in the City of Boston." Issued in Boston, MA, September 19.

Rose, D. and R. Warren (2001). *Police Use of Force Case Law: Instructor Guide*. Shawnee Mission, KS: Varro Press.

Ross, D.L. (2001). "Assessing the Impact of *Graham v. Conner* and *Canton v. Harris* Ten Years Later." Paper presented at the American Society of Law Enforcement Trainers (ASLET) Conference, Orlando, FL, February 16.

Schultz v. Long, 44 F.3rd 643 (8th Cir. 1995).

Scott v. Hendrich, 39 F 3rd 912 (9th Cir. 1994).

Scoville, D. (2000). "A View Askew: A Sideways Look at Racial Profiling." *Police Magazine,* 24(8)(August):16-23.

Siddle, B. (1999). "The Impact of the Sympathetic Nervous System on Use of Force Investigations." Milstadt, IL: PPCT Management Systems, Inc.

Skolnick, J.H. and J.J. Fyfe (1993). *Above the Law: Police and the Excessive Use of Force*. New York, NY: The Free Press.

Smith, D. (1980). "Police Attitudes and Performance: The Impact of Residency." *Urban Affairs Quarterly* 15(3):317-334.

Smith, R.W. (2001). "Death Notification: Breaking the News with Compassion for the Survivors and Concern for the Professionals." Seminar presentation in Cincinnati, Ohio, March 16.

Solomon, R.M. (2002). "Post-Shooting Trauma: Its Effects and Some Administrative Guidelines." Unpublished paper presented at the American Society for Law Enforcement Training (ASLET) annual conference on February 21.

Stone, M. (2002a). "Lethal Force and Law Enforcement Activity-Related Deaths — A Suggested Protocol for Investigation." *Training Bulletin* 5(2)(February):4.

—— (2002b). "The Trainer's Role in Lethal and Major Force Investigations and Litigation." Presentation to ASLET Conference, February 21.

Tennessee v. Garner, 471 U.S. 1 (1985).

Terrill, W. (2001). *Police Coercion: Application of the Force Continuum.* New York, NY: LFB Scholarly Publishing.

Thibault, E.A., L.M. Lynch and R.B. McBride (2001). *Proactive Police Management.* Saddle River, NJ: Prentice-Hall.

Thompson, G. (1983). *Verbal Judo: Words for Street Survival.* Springfield, IL: Charles Thomas.

Tong, E. (2001). "Teen Sues Police for Roughing in Arrest." *The Atlanta Journal-Constitution*, July 11.

Trojanowicz, R.C. (1989). *Preventing Civil Disturbances: A Community Policing Approach.* East Lansing, MI: The National Center for Community Policing, Michigan State University.

"Tucson Board Favors Riot Training Program" (2001). *Crime Control Digest*, September 21.

Tutko, T. and U. Tose (1976). *Sports Psyching: Playing Your Best Game All the Time.* New York, NY: Putnam Publishing.

U.S Department of Justice, Community Relations Service (2002). *Police Use of Force: Addressing Community Racial Tensions.* Washington, DC.

—— (2001a). "Memorandum of Agreement between the Department of Justice and the District of Columbia, Section II., #35." June 13, Washington, DC.

—— Civil Rights Division (2001b). *Report on Investigation of the Cincinnati Police Division.* Washington, DC.

—— (2001c). *Principles for Promoting Police Integrity.* Washington, DC.

—— (1999). *Use of Force by Police: Overview of National and Local Data.* (National Institute of Justice Research Report.) Washington, DC: NCJ 176330.

U.S. General Accounting Office (2000). *Racial Profiling: Limited Data Available on Motorist Stops.* Washington, DC.

U.S. National Institute of Justice (1999). *Use of Force by Police: Overview of National and Local Data.* Washington, DC: Research Report series (NCJ 176330).

—— (1994). *Oleoresin Capsicum: Pepper Spray as a Force Alternative.* Washington, DC: U.S. Department of Justice.

"U.S. Provides $7.5 Million in Cincinnati Settlement" (2002). *Crime Control Digest* 36(15), April 12.

Wadman, R. and S. Ziman (1993). "Courtesy and Police Authority." *FBI Law Enforcement Bulletin* 62(2)(February):23-26.

Walker, S. (2000). *Police Interactions with Racial and Ethnic Minorities: Assessing the Evidence and Allegations.* Washington, DC: Police Executive Research Forum.

—— G. Alpert and D. Kenney (2001). *Early Warning Systems: Responding to the Problem Police Officer.* Washington, DC: U.S. National Institute of Justice.

—— and B. Knight (1994). *Citizen Review of the Police, 1994.* Washington, DC: Police Executive Research Forum.

Weinblatt, R. (1999). "New Police Training Philosophy: Adult Learning Model on Verge of Nationwide Rollout." *Law and Order* (August):84-90.

White, M.D. (2001). "Controlling Police Decisions to Use Deadly Force: Reexamining the Importance of Administrative Policy." *Crime & Delinquency* 47(1):131-151.

Wood, R. (2003). "Police: Officer's Chase Proper." *The Cincinnati Post*, February 11.